Knit Noel™

Edited by Bobbie Matela

HOUSE of
WHITE
BIRCHES
PUBLISHERS
SINCE 1947

Knit Noel™

Editor	Bobbie Matela
Art Director	Brad Snow
Publishing Services Director	Brenda Gallmeyer
Associate Editor	Kathy Wesley
Assistant Art Director	Nick Pierce
Copy Supervisor	Michelle Beck
Copy Editors	Mary O'Donnell, Judy Weatherford
Technical Editor	Charlotte Quiggle
Technical Artist	Pam Gregory
Graphic Arts Supervisor	Ronda Bechinski
Graphic Artists	Jessi Butler, Minette Collins Smith
Production Assistant	Marj Morgan
Photography Supervisor	Tammy Christian
Photography	Don Clark, Matthew Owen, Jackie Schaffel
Photo Stylists	Tammy Smith, Tammy Steiner
Publishing Director	David J. McKee
Book Marketing Director	Dwight Seward

Printed in China
First Printing: 2007
Library of Congress Control Number: 2006933807
Hardcover ISBN: 978-1-59217-174-3
Softcover ISBN: 978-1-59217-196-5

Every effort has been made to ensure the accuracy and completeness of the instructions in this book.
However, we cannot be responsible for human error or for the results when using materials other than
those specified in the instructions, or for variations in individual work.

1 2 3 4 5 6 7 8 9

DRGbooks.com

Welcome

Knitting for the holidays is fun, energizing and lets those you love know how important they are!

As knitters, we make gifts and plans for the holidays all year round. No other time of the year lends itself to the colorful array of knitting possibilities. This volume is filled with a huge selection of seasonal delights and gift-giving ideas.

If you have ever wished that you had more time to create gifts, you'll appreciate our **Gifts in the Nick of Time**. These won't take all year to make; in fact, many are quick enough to create at the last minute.

Everyone should have the joy of a unique knitted stocking. Find the perfect modern or traditional style in our selection of **Stockings to Hang**. We've even included felted stockings!

For a wondrous holiday look, look to our **Deck the Halls, Trim the Tree** ideas. You'll love making these part of your holiday traditions.

Start now on cute sweaters for the babies and kids that still "believe." Find clever designs in our **Sweaters for Santa's Lap** chapter.

And one of the most appreciated gifts we can give ourselves or others are warm blankets. Make our **Winter Holiday Throws** in all sizes, from small lap-size to large enough to keep you warm while napping on the sofa.

You'll discover over 80 inspiring Knit Noel ideas by many of the foremost designers in the knitting world. They have enjoyed using Plymouth Yarns for all of our projects. We're sure you will love working with their yarns as well.

With warm thoughts,

Contents

Gifts in the Nick of Time

The Stockings to Hang

Deck the Halls, Trim the Trees

Sweaters for Santa's Lap

Winter Holiday Throws

Gifts in the Nick of Time

These gifts won't take all year to knit; in fact, many are quick enough to create at the last minute! Please the people on your gift list!

Merry Cables

This reversible scarf has a pretty edge, a big, braided center cable on one side and small mini-cables on the other. The results are smashing!

Design by Laura Andersson

Finished Size
6 inches wide; length as desired [samples are 44 (54, 72) inches]

Materials
- Cleckheaton Gusto 10 30 percent mohair/30 percent wool/40 percent acrylic super bulky weight yarn (56 yds/100g per ball): 3 balls pink #2101 (44-inch scarf); 4 balls aqua #2098 (54-inch scarf); 5 balls yellow #2099 (72-inch scarf)

  6 SUPER BULKY
- Size 11 (8mm) straight needles or size needed to obtain gauge
- Cable needle
- Tapestry needle

Gauge
11 sts and 14 rows = 4 inches/10cm in Seed St
To save time, take time to check gauge.

Special Abbreviations
RT (Right Twist): K2tog, leaving sts on LH needle; insert RH needle from the front between the 2 sts just knitted tog, and knit the first st again; sl both sts from the needle tog.

C6B (Cable 6 Back): Sl 3 to cn and hold in back, k3, k3 from cn.

C6F (Cable 6 Front): Sl 3 sts to cn and hold in Front, k3, k3 sts from cn.

Pattern Stitch
Seed St (odd number of sts)
Row 1: *K1, p1; rep from * to last st, end k1.
Rep Row 1 for Seed St.

Pattern Note
This scarf is reversible with a 9-st center cable on the "RS" and 2-st mini-cables at the sides on the "WS."

Scarf
Cast on 17 sts.

Edge
Work in Seed St for 2 inches, inc 5 sts evenly across last row. (23 sts)

Main scarf panel
Row 1 (RS): P1, k1, p2, k1, p2, k9, p2, k1, p2, k1, p1.
Row 2 and all WS rows: K1, p1, RT, p1, k2, p9, k2, p1, RT, p1, k1.
Row 3: P1, k1, p2, k1, p2, C6F, k3, p2, k1, p2, k1, p1.
Row 5: Rep Row 1.
Row 7: P1, k1, p2, k1, p2, k3, C6B, p2, k1, p2, k1, p1.
Row 8: Rep Row 2.
  Rep Rows 1–8 until scarf is 2 inches short of desired length, ending with Row 1 or 5.

Edge
Next row (WS): Work in Seed St, dec 5 sts evenly across first row in pat. (17 sts)
  Continue in Seed St for 2 inches. Bind off in pat.

Finishing
Weave in all ends.
  Gently hand-wash the scarf in lukewarm water and dry flat. ❇

In the Spirit Scarf

Your favorite sports fan will cheer in warmth and style wearing a scarf custom-knit in her team's colors.

Design by Lois S. Young

Finished Size
9½ x 70 inches (excluding fringe)

Materials

- Plymouth Tweed 100 percent virgin lamb's wool medium weight yarn (109 yds/50g per ball): 4 balls purple #5316 (MC); 1 ball each of orange #5327 (A) and blue #5325 (B)
- Size 7 (4.5mm) needles or size needed to obtain gauge
- Size E/4 (3.5mm) crochet hook (for attaching fringe)
- Tapestry needle

Gauge
21 sts and 25 rows = 4 inches/10cm in pat st
To save time, take time to check gauge.

Pattern Stitch
Broken Rib Pattern (multiple of 6 sts + 3)
Row 1: *P3, k3, rep from *, end p3.
Row 2: *K1, p1, rep from *, end k1.
Rep Rows 1 and 2 for pat.

Pattern Notes
Pat is reversible.
Cut yarn with 3-inch tail at each color change.

Scarf
With MC, cast on 51 sts.
Work 4 rows of pat st.
Change colors as follows:
4 rows A
4 rows MC
4 rows B

18 rows MC
[Rep sequence] 6 times.
Reverse A and B stripes:
4 rows B
4 rows MC
4 rows A
18 rows MC
[Rep sequence] 5 times.
4 rows B
4 rows MC
4 rows A
4 rows MC
Bind off loosely in pat.

Fringe
Cut 68 (9-inch) strands of MC. Referring to instructions on page 173, make Single Knot Fringe, using 2 strands for each knot; tie knots every 3 sts across each short edge. Trim even.
Weave in all ends.
Block, if necessary. ✳

Add a Little Glitter

Dress up any coat with this sparkly, fuzzy scarf!

■■□□ EASY

Design by Cindy Adams

Finished Size

8 x 72 inches (excluding fringe)

Materials

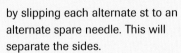

- Plymouth Tomorrow 40 percent nylon/38 percent mohair/18 percent acrylic/4 percent metal bulky weight yarn (82 yds/50g per ball): 5 balls green/blue/brown/gray #1607
- Size 11 (8mm) straight needles or size needed to obtain gauge
- 2 spare needles of any size
- Size H/8 (5mm) crochet hook (for adding fringe)
- Tapestry needle

Gauge

10 sts and 11 rows = 4 inches/10cm in double-knit st (measured on 1 side)
To save time, take time to check gauge.

Pattern Notes

This scarf is worked in double-knit, resulting in a tubular piece of fabric; each row of fabric requires 2 rows of knitting.

For ease of knitting, this scarf is worked inside out, then turned right side out before binding off.

Scarf

Cut 80 pieces of yarn, each 14 inches long. Set aside in a bag (or other safe place) for fringe.

Cast on 40 sts.

Row 1: *P1, sl 1 purlwise; rep from * across.

Rep Row 1 until there are about 2 yds left in last ball of yarn.

Divide sts onto 2 spare needles by slipping each alternate st to an alternate spare needle. This will separate the sides.

Turn scarf right side out. Weave in all ends on WS.

Rejoin the sides by slipping sts alternately from spare needles back to original needle.

Bind off in the normal manner. This will make both ends the same width, which is slightly wider than the scarf.

Fringe

*Fold 1 fringe in half. With RS facing and beg at first knit st of lower edge, use crochet hook to draw folded end from RS to WS through st. Pull loose ends through folded section. Draw knot up firmly. Rep from *, placing 1 fringe in every knit st across. Turn scarf over to other side and rep. (40 fringes along bottom edge)

Rep on other end. Trim fringes even. ❋

Luscious Warmth

Gradual color changes and loopy mohair yarn add
a touch of elegance to this easy-to-knit lacy scarf.

◼◼◻◻ EASY

Design by Pauline Schultz

Finished Size
Approx 5 x 80 inches (excluding fringe)

Materials
- Plymouth Today 80 percent mohair/15 percent wool/5 percent nylon bulky weight yarn (100 yds/50g per ball): 2 balls orange/burgundy #1663
- Size 11 (8mm) 36-inch circular needle
- Size J/10 (6mm) crochet hook
- Tapestry needle

Gauge
Gauge is not critical.

Pattern Note
Pat is worked back and forth; a circular needle is used to accommodate the large number of sts.

Scarf
Using long-tail method, cast on 190 sts.
Row 1 (RS): Yo, knit to last 2 sts, k2tog.
Row 2: Skp, knit to last st; knit and purl into last st.
Rows 3 and 4: Rep Rows 1 and 2.
Row 5: K1, *yo, k2tog; rep from * to last st, k1.
Row 6: Skp, *yo, k2tog; rep from * to last 2 sts, yo, k2.
[Rep Rows 1–6] twice. Rep Rows 1–4. Bind off loosely.

Fringe
Loosely work a row of single crochet along each end to form a base for the fringe.
Cut 60 (12-inch) strands of yarn. Referring to instructions on page 173, make Single Knot Fringe, using 6 strands for each knot; tie 5 knots evenly spaced across each short end. Trim fringe ends on the diagonal.

Finishing
Weave in all ends.
Gently hand-wash the scarf in lukewarm water and dry flat. ❄

Tie-It-On Scarf or Belt

Wrap yourself up as pretty as a present in this multi-colored knit accessory.

■■□□ EASY

Design by Anita Closic

Finished Size

3 x 60 inches

Materials

- Plymouth Hand Paint Wool 100 percent wool super bulky weight yarn (60 yds/ 100g per skein): 1 skein vivid multi #15

  6 SUPER BULKY
- Size 15 (10mm) 32-inch circular needle or size needed to obtain gauge
- Tapestry needle

Gauge

8 sts and 16 rows = 4 inches/10cm in garter st
To save time, take time to check gauge.

Belt

Using long-tail cast-on method, *cast on 3 sts, yo; rep from * 25 times, end cast on 3. (107 sts, including yos)

Work 7 rows in garter st.

Row 8: *K3, drop next st off needle and ravel 1 row down, pick up horizontal strand above st just dropped with RH needle and knit; rep from * to last 3 sts, k3.

Row 9: Bind off loosely.

Finishing

Ravel all dropped sts down to yo on cast-on edge.

Weave in all ends. ❋

Fascinating Hat & Hand Warmers

Delicate lace pairs with soft warm alpaca for this lovely hat and hand-warmer set.

◼◼◼◻ INTERMEDIATE

Designs by Celeste Pinheiro

Size
Woman's average

Finished Measurements
Hat: 21-inch circumference
Hand warmers: 7 inches around x 8½ inches long

Materials
- Plymouth Baby Alpaca Worsted 100 percent baby alpaca medium weight yarn (102 yds/ 50g per ball): 3 skeins pink #5605
- Size 6 (4mm) straight needles
- Size 8 (5mm) straight and double-pointed needles or size needed to obtain gauge
- Tapestry needle

Gauge
20 sts and 24 rows = 4 inches/10cm in St st with larger needles
To save time, take time to check gauge.

Special Abbreviations
MB (Make Bobble): [K1, p1, k1 p1] into st, pass first 3 sts over last st.
Sk2p (left-leaning double dec): Sl 1, k2tog, psso.

Pattern Stitch
Lace Stripe (multiple of 8 sts)
Row 1 (RS): With larger needle, *k2tog, yo; rep from *.
Row 2 and all WS rows (except where noted): Purl.
Row 3: Knit.

Row 5: Change to smaller needles and knit.

Rows 6–8: Knit.

Row 9: Change to larger needles and knit.

Row 11: *K3, yo, ssk, k3; rep from * across.

Row 13: *K1, k2tog, yo, k1, yo, ssk, k2; rep from * across.

Row 15: *K2tog, yo, k3, yo, ssk, k1; rep from * across.

Row 17: *K2, yo, sk2p, yo, k3; rep from *.

Row 19: *K3, yo, ssk, k3; rep from *.

Row 21: Change to smaller needles and knit.

Rows 22–24: Knit.

Row 25: Change to larger needles and knit.

Row 27: *MB, k3; rep from * across.

Row 29: Knit.

Row 31: Change to smaller needles and knit.

Rows 32–34: Knit.

Row 35: Change to larger needles and knit.

Row 37: *Yo, ssk, k6; rep from * across.

Row 39: *K1, yo, ssk, k3, k2tog, yo; rep from * across.

Row 41: *K2, yo, ssk, k1, k2tog, yo, k1; rep from * across.

Row 43: *K3, yo, sk2p, yo, k2; rep from * across.

Row 45: *K4, yo, ssk, k2; rep from * across.

Row 47: Knit.

Row 49: Change to smaller needles and knit.

Rows 50–52: Knit.

Pattern Note

The first and last st of each row are selvage sts; work in St st throughout, working all patterning and shaping within these 2 sts.

Hat

With larger needles, cast on 106 sts. Work 9 rows in St st, ending with a WS row.

Next row (RS): K1 (selvage st), work Row 1 Lace Stripe pat to last st, end k1 (selvage st).

Continue working Lace Stripe pat, maintaining selvage sts in St st and ending with Row 28.

Shape crown

Setup Row: K1 (selvage st), *k11, k2tog, place marker; rep from * to last st, end k1 (selvage st). (98 sts)

Next row: Purl.

Dec row 1 (RS): *Knit to 2 sts before marker, k2tog; rep from * to end of row, end k1.

Rep last 2 rows until 34 sts rem, ending with a RS row.

Dec row 2 (WS): P1, *p2tog, purl to

marker; rep from * to last st, end p1. (26 sts)

Rep Dec rows 1 and 2. (10 sts)

Cut yarn, leaving a 5-inch tail.

Using tapestry needle, thread tail through rem sts, and pull tight.

Weave in all ends.

Finishing
Sew seam.

Hand Warmers
Right hand
With larger needles, cast on 34 sts. Change to smaller needles and knit 3 rows.

Change to larger needles.

Next row (RS): K1 (selvage st), work Row 1 Lace Stripe pat to last st, end k1 (selvage st).

Continue working Lace Stripe pat, ending with Row 52 and maintaining selvage sts in St st.

Thumbhole row (RS): K1, work 16 sts of Row 1 of Lace Stripe pat, bind off 5 sts, k1, continue with Lace Stripe pat as established to last st, end k1.

Next row (WS): P1, work Row 2 of Lace Stripe pat, casting on 5 sts over bound-off sts of previous row.

Work Rows 3–10 of Lace Stripe pat.

Next row (RS): K1, work Row 27 of Lace Stripe pat over next 16 sts, knit to end.

Work Rows 28–34 of Lace Stripe pat, maintaining selvage sts.

Change to larger needles and bind off loosely.

Thumb
With dpns, pick up and knit 14 sts around thumb hole.

Knit 6 rnds.

Purl 1 rnd.

Bind off loosely.

Left hand
Work as for right hand to Thumbhole.

Thumbhole row (RS): K1, work 10 sts of Row 1 of Lace Stripe pat, bind off 5 sts, k1, continue with Lace Stripe pat as established to last st, end k1.

Next row (WS): P1, work Row 2 of Lace Stripe pat, casting on 5 sts over bound-off sts of previous row.

Work Rows 3–10 of Lace Stripe pat.

Next row (RS): K1, k16, work Row 27 of Lace Stripe pat over next 16 sts, end k1.

Work Rows 28–34 of Lace Stripe pat, maintaining selvage sts.

Change to larger needles and bind off loosely.

Work thumb as for right hand.

Finishing
Sew side seams. ❄

Beaded Cable Head Cozy

This elegant little headband uses a sparkly alpaca yarn, beads, and a wavy cable pattern.

▆▆▆▭ INTERMEDIATE

Design by Christine L. Walter

Finished Size
19-inch circumference x 3¼ inches wide

Materials
- Plymouth Baby Alpaca Worsted Glow 97 percent baby alpaca/3 percent Stellina medium weight yarn (102 yds/50g per ball): 1 ball chartreuse #3843
- Size 8 (5mm) straight needles or size needed to obtain gauge
- Size H/8 (5mm) crochet hook
- 24 Mill Hill Pebble Beads size 3/0 gold #05557
- Large-eye beading needle
- Tapestry needle

Gauge
20 sts and 28 rows = 4 inches/10cm in St st
To save time, take time to check gauge.

Special Abbreviations
BUB (Bring Up Bead): Slide 1 bead up and work next st as indicated.
C6F (Cable 6 Front): Sl 3 sts to cn and hold in front, k3, k3 from cn.
C6B (Cable 6 Back): Sl 3 sts to cn and hold in back, k3, k3 from cn.

Pattern Stitch
Wavy Cable
Row 1 (RS): K13, p2, BUB, p2, k3.
Row 2: K7, p10, k3.
Row 3: K7, C6F, p4, k3.
Row 4: K3, p10, k7.
Row 5: K3, p4, k13.
Row 6: Rep Row 4.
Row 7: K3, p2, BUB, p2, k13.
Row 8: Rep Row 4.
Row 9: K3, p4, C6B, k7.
Row 10: Rep Row 2.
Row 11: K13, p4, k3.
Row 12: Rep Row 2.
Rep Rows 1–12 for pat.

Pattern Notes
The instructions below are to cast on and bind off normally and sew the ends tog. More experienced knitters may prefer to provisionally cast on and end knitting on Row 11, then graft the end sts tog in pat on Row 12.

A chart for the Wavy Cable pat is included for those preferring to work from a chart.

Headband
Pre-string 24 Pebble beads onto project yarn.

Cast on 20 sts.

Work Wavy Cable pat 12 times or until piece measures approx 19 inches, ending on Row 12.

Bind off loosely.

Cut yarn leaving a 20-inch tail.

Use tail to sew ends tog.

Finishing
Weave in ends.

Block lightly. ❊

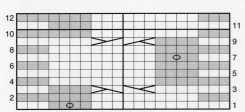

WAVY CABLE

STITCH KEY
☐ K on RS, p on WS
▨ P on RS, k on WS
⬭ P1, BUB, p1
⟩⟨ C6F
⟩⟨ C6B

Fair Isle With Flair Set

Give someone special this super-warm, fleece-lined headband and matching bag.

⬤⬤⬤▭ INTERMEDIATE

Designs by Gayle Bunn

Finished Measurements
Bag: 12 inches wide x 10½ inches high
Headband: 21 inches around x 4 inches wide

Materials
- Plymouth Galway Worsted  100 percent wool medium weight yarn (210 yds/100g per ball): 2 balls purple #15 (MC); 1 ball each teal #139 (A), salmon #157 (B) and lime #146 (C)
- Size 8 (5mm) straight needles or size needed to obtain gauge
- Size 7 (4.5mm) 24-inch circular needle
- Approx ½ yard fleece fabric in coordinating color for lining
- Matching sewing thread
- Sewing needle
- 1¾-inch toggle
- Tapestry needle

Gauge
20 sts and 26 rows = 4 inches/10cm in stranded St st with larger needles
  To save time, take time to check gauge.

Pattern Note
For bag, beg Chart D on RS row; for headband, begin Chart D on WS row.

Bag
Front
**With larger needles and MC, cast on 55 sts.
  Beg with a RS row, work 6 rows St st, inc 4 sts evenly across last row. (59 sts)
    Work Chart A.
    Work Chart B.
    Work Chart C.
Next row (WS): With MC, purl dec 4 sts evenly across. (55 sts)

Work even in St st for 10 rows.
Next row: Continue in St st dec 1 st each side. (53 sts)
  Work even in St st for 7 rows.
Next row: Continue in St st dec 1 st each side.** (51 sts)
  Work even until piece measures 9½ inches, ending with a RS row.
  Knit 2 rows.
  Bind off knitwise on WS.

Back
Work from ** to ** as for Front.
  Work even until piece measures 10 inches, ending with a WS row.
  Place markers at each end of last row.

Flap
Work even for 10 rows.
  Work Chart D, and *at the same time*, dec 1 st each end of Row 5 and [every RS row] 8 times. (33 sts)
  With MC, continue in St st dec 1 st each end [every RS row] 3 times. (27 sts)
  Purl 1 row.
  Bind off.

Finishing
Pin pieces flat and cover with a damp cloth, or steam lightly on WS.
  Using front as guide, cut 2 pieces of lining fabric (fleece) with ⅜-inches seam allowance around all edges.

Flap Edging
With circular needle and MC, beg at right marker on back, pick up and knit

Lining

Machine- or hand-stitch sides and bottom seam of lining.

Press ⅜ inch along top edge to WS.

Place inside bag and sew top edge in position.

Twisted Cord Strap

Cut 2 strands of MC approx 6 yds long. Fold in half and secure folded end to a stationary object. Twist yarn until it begins to double back on itself. Fold in half again with both ends tog and allow to twist up on itself. Cut to 43 inches or desired length and knot the ends to secure. Attach each end to sides of bag where flap edging and outer edging join.

Button Loop

Cut 1 strand of MC approx 12 inches long. Make twisted cord as above. Cut to 2½ inches, fold in half and sew securely to center edge of flap.

Sew toggle in position opposite button loop.

Headband

With larger needles, MC and long-tail method, cast on 97 sts.

Knit 2 rows.

Next row (WS): Knit, inc 7 sts evenly across. (104 sts)

Next row: Knit.

Next row (WS): P1 MC, work [6-st rep of Chart D] 17 times, p1 MC.

Complete Chart D, working first and last sts on each row with MC.

Next row (RS): With MC, knit, dec 7 sts evenly across. (97 sts)

Knit 2 rows.

Bind off knitwise on WS.

Finishing

Pin piece flat and cover with a damp cloth, or steam lightly on WS.

Lining

Cut lining fabric (fleece) to measure same length and width as headband. Turn under both long sides of lining to WS ⅜ inches. With matching thread and sewing needle, sew long sides of lining to WS of Headband. Sew center back seam of headband and lining. ❄

31 sts along shaped side of flap to bind off edge, 25 sts across bind-off edge and 31 sts along shaped side to opposite marker. (87 sts)

Knit 1 row.

Next row: Knit, inc 1 st at each corner of flap. (89 sts)

Bind off knitwise on WS.

Outer Edging

With circular needle and MC, beg at top edge of Front, pick up and knit 46 sts down side of front, 2 sts in corner, 53 sts across cast on edge, 2 sts in corner and 46 sts up opposite side. (103 sts)

Knit 1 row.

Next row: Knit, inc 1 st at each corner. (105 sts)

Bind off knitwise on WS.

Sew back to front along sides and across lower edge, leaving outer edging free. Sew sides of Flap Edging to Outer Edging at fold line of flap.

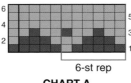

6-st rep
CHART A

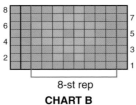

8-st rep
CHART B

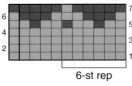

6-st rep
CHART C

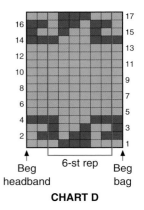

Beg headband — 6-st rep — Beg bag

CHART D

COLOR KEY
- ■ Purple (MC)
- ▨ Teal (A)
- ▨ Salmon (B)
- ▨ Lime (C)

Family Fun Mittens

These textured, waffle-rib mittens will keep your family's hands nice and toasty this winter. Make a pair in each size to keep in the car for emergencies, or make a pair for your child's favorite teacher.

■■■□ INTERMEDIATE

Design by Christine L. Walter

Sizes

Child's (woman's, man's) Instructions are given for smallest size, with larger sizes in parentheses. When only 1 number is given, it applies to all sizes.

Finished Measurements

Hand circumference: 6 (8, 9) inches

Materials

• Plymouth Galway Worsted Marl 100 percent wool medium weight yarn (210 yds/100g per ball): 1 ball of salmon mix #602 (child's) or turquoise mix #603 (woman's/man's)
• Size 6 (4mm) double-pointed needles or size needed to obtain gauge
• Stitch markers (1 in CC for beg of rnd)
• Tapestry needle

4 MEDIUM

Gauge

23 sts and 30 rows = 4 inches/10cm in Waffle Rib pat (blocked)
To save time, take time to check gauge.

Special Abbreviations

M1L (Make 1 Left): Insert LH needle from front to back under the horizontal strand between the last st worked and next st on left needle. With RH needle, knit into the back of this loop.
M1R (Make 1 Right): Insert LH needle from back to front under the horizontal strand between the last st worked and next st on left needle. With RH needle, knit into the front of this loop.
Pm (Place Marker): Place marker on needle.

Inc (Increase): Knit in front and back of st to inc 1 st.

Pattern Stitch

Waffle Rib (multiple of 5 sts)

Rnds 1 and 2: Knit.
Rnds 3–6: *K1, p3, k1; rep from * to end.
　Rep Rows 1–6 for pat.

Mittens

Cuff

Cast on 30 (40, 50) sts. Distribute evenly on 3 or 4 dpn and join without twisting; pm between first and last sts.

Work in k1, p1 rib until cuff measures 2¼ (2¾, 3) inches.

Thumb Gusset

Work Rnd 1 of Waffle Rib across 15 (20, 25) sts, pm, k1, pm, continue in pat to last st, inc1. (31, 41, 51 sts)

Inc rnd: Work in pat to first marker, sl marker; M1L, knit to next marker, M1R, sl marker; work in pat to end of rnd.

Rep Inc rnd [every 3rd rnd] 2 (5, 7) times, then [every 4th rnd] 2 (1, 0) times. (11, 15, 17 sts between markers)

Next rnd: Work in pat to first marker, place sts between markers on a piece of waste yarn (removing markers), cast on 1 st over gap left by gusset, work in pat to end of rnd. (31, 41, 51 sts)

Hand

Next rnd: Work in pat as established, knitting the st cast on over gusset.

Next rnd: Work 15 (20, 25) sts in pat, k2tog, work in pat to end of rnd. (30, 40, 50 sts)

Work even until piece measures approx 3½ (5¾, 6¾) inches from top of ribbing.

Next rnd: Work 15 (20, 25) sts in pat, pm, work to end of rnd.

Shape Top

Dec rnd: *Ssk, work in pat as established to 2 sts before marker, k2tog, sl marker; rep from *. (26, 36, 46 sts)

Next rnd: *K1, work in pat to 1 st before marker, k1; rep from *.

[Rep last 2 rnds] 3 (4, 6) times. (14, 20, 22 sts)

Next rnd: *Ssk, knit to 2 sts before marker, k2tog, sl marker; rep from *. (10, 16, 18 sts)

[Rep last rnd] 1 (2, 3) time(s). (6, 8, 6 sts)

Thumb

Place 11 (15, 17) gusset sts onto 3 dpn; pick up and knit 1 st over gap and join; pm for beg of rnd. (12, 16, 18 sts)

Work in St st until thumb measures approx 1 (1¾, 2) inches from pick-up rnd.

Next rnd: [K4 (5, 6), pm] twice, k4 (6, 6).

Shape Top

Dec rnd: [Knit to 2 sts before marker, k2tog] around. (9, 13, 15 sts)

Rep Dec rnd [every (every other, every other) rnd] 1 (2, 2) time(s). (6, 7, 9 sts)

Largest size only
Rep Dec rnd. (6 sts)

All sizes
Cut yarn, leaving a 5-inch tail.

Using tapestry needle, thread tail through rem sts and pull tight.

Finishing

Weave in ends.
Block lightly. ❋

Not-Your-Basic Beanie

This beautiful, textured hat will suit both men and women—anyone on your list would be thrilled to receive such a luxurious gift.

Design by Christine L. Walter

Size
Adult average

Finished Measurement
Circumference: 18 inches

Materials
• Plymouth Super Taj Majal 70 percent super fine merino/22 percent silk/8 percent cashmere medium weight yarn (127 yds/50g per ball): 2 balls rust #1436

• Size 7 (4.5mm) 16-inch circular and double-pointed needles or size needed to obtain gauge
• Stitch marker
• Tapestry needle

Gauge
24 sts and 30 rows = 4 inches/10cm in Mock Wave Cable
23 sts and 31 rows = 4 inches/10cm in Carved Diamond pat
To save time, take time to check gauge.

Special Abbreviations
RT (Right Twist): K2tog, leaving sts on LH needle; insert RH needle from the front between the 2 sts just knitted tog, and knit the first st again; sl both sts from the needle tog.

LT (Left Twist): With RH needle behind LH needle, skip 1 st and knit the 2nd st through the back loop; insert RH needle into the backs of both sts (the skipped st and the 2nd st) and k2tog-tbl.

CDD (Centered Double Decrease): Sl next 2 sts as if to k2tog, k1, p2sso.

Pattern Stitches
A. Mock Wave Cable (multiple of 4 sts)
Rnds 1–3: *P2, k2; rep from * to end of rnd.
Rnd 4: *P2, LT; rep from * to end of rnd.
Rnds 5–7: *P2, k2; rep from * to end of rnd.
Rnd 8: *P2, RT; rep from * to end of rnd.
Rep Rnds 1–8 for pat.

B. Carved Diamond (multiple of 16 sts)
Rnd 1 and all odd-numbered rnds: Knit.
Rnd 2: *K1, [RT] 3 times, k1, [LT] 3 times, k2; rep from * around.
Rnd 4: *[RT] 3 times, k3, [LT] 3 times, k1; rep from * around.
Rnds 6–8: Rep Rnds 2-4.
Rnd 10: Knit.
Rnd 12: *[LT] 3 times, k3, [RT] 3 times, k1; rep from * around.
Rnd 14: *K1, [LT] 3 times, k1, [RT] 3 times, k2; rep from * around.
Rnds 16–18: Rep Rnds 12-14.
Rnd 20: Knit.
  Rep Rnds 1–20 for pat.

Pattern Notes
Cuff is worked inside out, then knitting direction changes so that body is worked right side out.

Change to dpns when sts no longer fit comfortably on circular needle.

A chart for the Carved Diamond pat is included for those preferring to work from a chart.

Hat
Cuff
Cast on 96 sts. Join without twisting; place marker between first and last sts.

Work 3 reps of Mock Wave Cable pat, then work Rnds 1 and 2.

Reverse knitting direction for body of hat as follows: sl first st purlwise from LH needle to RH needle, bring yarn to front, return st by slipping it purlwise back to the LH needle. First st is wrapped to prevent hole. Turn work, sl marker, and beg body.

Body
Change to Carved Diamond pat and work Rnds 1–20, then Rnds 1–19.

Continued on page 53

Quick Eyeglasses Case

This little eyeglasses case uses a variegated yarn and an easy, woven stitch that results in an attractive tweedy effect. Make it in one day when you need a quick gift!

■■■□ INTERMEDIATE

Design by Christine L. Walter

Finished Size
7 inches wide x 3 inches tall

Materials
- Plymouth Outback Wool 100 percent virgin wool medium weight yarn (370 yds/200g per skein): 1 skein of caramel mix #915
- Size 8 (5mm) double-pointed needles (set of 5) or size needed to obtain gauge
- Size E/4 (3.5mm) crochet hook
- Stitch marker
- Tapestry needle
- Large hook-and-eye closure
- Sharp sewing needle
- Thread to match yarn

Gauge
19 sts and 30 rows = 4 inches/10cm in Woven Stitch pat

To save time, take time to check gauge.

Pattern Stitch
Woven St (even number of sts)
Rnd 1: Knit.
Rnd 2: *K1, sl 1 wyif; rep from * across.
Rnd 3: Knit.
Rnd 4: *Sl 1 wyif, k1; rep from * across.
Rep Rows 1–4 for pat.

Eyeglasses Case
Cast on 28 sts.

Knit 5 rows; after last row, do not turn.

With 2nd dpn, pick up and knit 3 sts along edge on left side of work; with 3rd dpn, pick up and knit 28 sts along cast-on edge; with 4th dpn, pick up and knit 3 sts along edge on right side of work. (62 sts)

Join and place marker between first and last sts.

Work 3 reps of Woven St pat, then work Rnds 1 and 2.

Next rnd: Bind off 28 sts purlwise and remove marker. (34 sts)

Flap
Beg working back and forth.
Row 1 (RS): P1, p2tog, purl to last 3 sts, p2tog, p1. (32 sts)
Row 2: Purl.
Rep [Rows 1 and 2] 5 times. Rep Row 1. (20 sts)

Cut yarn, leaving a 6-inch tail.

Flap Edging
With crochet hook and back side of case facing you and beg at right edge of flap, work a sl st for each garter ridge up to live sts at top of flap. Using the lp on hook as first knit st, bind off across top of flap. Sl rem lp back to crochet hook and work sl st down the opposite side of the flap, stopping at the left edge of front. Cut yarn.

Finishing
Weave in ends.

Block lightly.

Referring to photo, with matching thread, sew on hook and eye. ❄

Good Cheer Bottle Cozy

When you bring your party hostess a bottle of wine, dress it up in this pretty gift bag.

◼◼◻◻ EASY

Design by Donna Druchunas

Finished Size
8 inch circumference x 16 inches tall, with ribbing slightly stretched

Materials
- Plymouth Galway Worsted 100 percent wool medium weight yarn (210 yds/100g per ball): 1 ball each bright pink #137 (MC), orange #154 (A) and white #8 (B) **[4 MEDIUM]**
- Size 6 (4mm) double-pointed needles
- Size 8 (5mm) double-pointed needles or size needed to obtain gauge
- Size H/8 (5mm) crochet hook
- Stitch marker
- Tapestry needle

Gauge
24 sts and 22 rows = 4 inches/10cm in K1, P1 Rib (slightly stretched) on larger needles

To save time, take time to check gauge.

Pattern Stitch
K1, P1 Rib (even number of sts)
All rnds: *K1, p1; rep from * around.

Wine Bag
With smaller needles and MC, cast on 48 sts. Distribute sts evenly on 3 or 4 dpns. Join without twisting; place marker between first and last sts.

Work in K1, P1 Rib until piece measures 2 inches.

Eyelet rnd: *Ssk, yo; rep from * around.

Next rnd: *K1, purl into yo; rep from * around.

Change to larger needles.

Continue in K1, P1 Rib until bag measures 15 inches.

Bottom
Rnd 1 (and all odd rounds): Knit.
Rnd 2: *K4, k2tog; rep from * around. (40 sts)
Rnd 4: *K3, k2tog; rep from * around. (32 sts)
Rnd 6: *K2, k2tog; rep from * around. (24 sts)
Rnd 8: *K1, k2tog; rep from * around. (16 sts)
Rnd 10: K2tog around. (8 sts)

Cut yarn, leaving an 8-inch tail. Using tapestry needle, thread tail through rem sts, and pull tight.

Finishing
Ruffles
With crochet hook, attach A to a purl st 2 rows below any eyelet.

Ruffle rnd: *Ch 16, skip 1 eyelet, then sl st to the purl st 2 rows below next eyelet. Rep from *, attaching the chain to the purl st 2 rows below every other eyelet until you join the ruffle to the original purl st. Fasten off and pull yarn tails inside bag.

Attach B to a purl st 2 rows below 1 of the eyelets skipped on first Ruffle rnd.

Rep Ruffle rnd, attaching chain below the eyelets skipped when making first ruffle.

Make a 2nd set of ruffles approx 2 inches below the first, attaching chain to every other purl st in rib.

Weave in all ends on WS.

Drawstring
Make 2 (24-inch) crochet chains, 1 each in A and B.

Weave in and out of eyelets and tie in a bow.

Wash and dry flat to block. ✳

Soothing Spa Set

Made from a blend of linen and cotton, this delicate lace-patterned spa set is sturdy enough to use in any shower (or bath).

BEGINNER

Designs by Celeste Pinheiro

Finished Sizes

Face cloth: 10 inches wide x 11 inches long
Soap pouch: 3½ inches wide x 6 inches long
Back scrubber: 5 inches wide x 24 inches long (not including handles)

Materials

- Plymouth Linen Isle 50 percent cotton/30 percent rayon/20 percent linen medium weight yarn (86 yds/50g per ball): 5 balls sea foam #8699
- Size 6 (4mm) straight needles
- Size 9 (5.5mm) straight needles or size needed to obtain gauge
- 4 (1-inch) pearl buttons

4 MEDIUM

Gauge

20 sts and 40 rows = 4 inches/10cm in garter st with smaller needles
16 st and 32 rows = 4 inches/10cm in garter st with larger needles and 2 strands of yarn held tog.
To save time, take time to check gauge.

Pattern Stitch

Garter Eyelet (odd number of sts)
Rows 1–3: Knit.
Rows 4 and 8 (RS): *K2tog, yo; rep from * to last st, k1.
Rows 5–7: Knit.
Rows 9–12: Knit.
   Rep Rows 1–12 for pat.

Pattern Note

Face cloth and soap pouch are worked with single strand of yarn; the back scrubber is worked with 2 strands of yarn held tog.

Face Cloth

With smaller needles, cast on 51 sts.
   Work 8 reps of Garter Eyelet pat.
   Knit 1 row.
   Bind off.

Soap Pouch

With smaller needles, cast on 35 sts.
   Work 4 reps of Garter Eyelet pat.
   Knit 3 rows.
   Bind off.

Finishing

Fold in half lengthwise; sew bottom and side seams.
   Cut 6 strands 20 inches long. Hold the 6 strands tog and knot at 1 end.
   With 2 strands held tog, make a 3-strand braid.
   Thread braid through eyelet row. Cut first knot, then join both ends tog with an overhand knot.
   Trim ends even.

Back scrubber

With larger needles and 2 strands of yarn held tog, cast on 21 sts.
   Work 12 reps of Garter Eyelet pat.
   Knit 1 row.
   Bind off.

Handles

Make 2
With larger needles and 2 strands yarn held tog, cast on 6 sts.
   Work in garter st for 9 inches.
   Bind off.
   Sew ends of 1 handle to 1 end of scrubber. Rep for 2nd handle.
   Sew 1 button over each join of handle and scrubber as shown in photo.
   Wash and block pieces, pinning slightly to prevent the fabric from biasing. ❄

Striped Gift Baskets

Why box your gifts? Put soaps (or other goodies) in these felted baskets for a made-to-order personalized present.

■■■□ INTERMEDIATE

Design by Donna Druchunas

Size
Small (large) Instructions are given for smaller size, with larger size in parentheses. When only 1 number is given, it applies to both sizes.

Finished Felted Measurements
Approx 4 (5) inches tall x 18 (24)-inch top circumference

Materials
- Plymouth Galway Chunky 100 percent wool bulky weight yarn (123 yds/100g per ball): 1 ball each of lime #146 (A), aqua #149 (B), and fuchsia #141 (C)
- Size 15 (10mm) 16-inch circular and double-pointed needles or size needed to obtain gauge
- Tapestry needle
- Top-loading washing machine, zippered pillowcase, and laundry soap for felting

Pre-Felted Gauge
9 sts and 12 rows = 4 inches/10cm in St st Exact gauge is not critical; make sure your sts are loose and airy.

Stripe Sequence
*Knit 4 rnds A, 2 rnds B, 2 rnds C, 2 rnds B, 2 rnds C.
   Rep from * for Stripe pat.

Pattern Notes
Cut each yarn at end of stripe; do not carry up.
   Change to dpns when sts no longer fit comfortably on circular needle.

Measurements are achieved using yarn and colors specified; results may vary depending on yarn, yarn color and felting time.
   If solid-colored baskets are preferred, 1 ball of yarn will make a basket of each size.

Baskets
With circular needle and C, cast on 60 (75) sts. Join without twisting; place marker between first and last sts.
   Knit 2 rnds.
   Work in Stripe pat until piece measures 6 (10) inches.

Shape Bottom
Continue in Stripe pat, and dec as follows:
Setup rnd: *K12 (15), place marker; rep from * around.

Rnd 1: *Ssk, knit to 2 sts before marker, k2tog; rep from * around. (50, 65 sts)
Rnds 2: Knit.
   Rep [Rnds 1 and 2] 3 times. (30, 35 sts)
   Rep [Rnd 1] twice. (10, 15 sts)
   Cut yarn, leaving a 5-inch tail. Using tapestry needle, thread tail through rem sts, and pull tight.
   Weave in all ends.

Felting
Felt following Felting instructions on page 172 until baskets reach finished measurements or desired size then gently rinse in the sink. Roll the baskets in a towel and squeeze out the excess water.
   Shape over a bowl or shape with hands and leave to dry. ※

Fashionably Fringed Tote

This lightly felted tote is just the thing for holding your knitting projects or for carrying things to and from the office.

Design by Posey Salem

Finished Felted Measurements

14 inches wide x 12 inches high x 4 inches deep

Materials

- Plymouth Hand Paint Wool 100 percent wool super bulky weight yarn (60 yds/100g per skein): 8 skeins rose multi #170
- Size 11 (8mm) double-pointed needles
- Size 15 (10mm) 24-inch and 29-inch circular needles or size needed to obtain gauge
- 2 stitch markers (1 in CC for beg of rnd)
- Large crochet hook (for fringe)
- Tapestry needle
- 1 yd of cotton thread or yarn
- Top-loading washing machine, zippered pillowcase, and laundry soap for felting

Pre-Felted Gauge

9½ sts and 13 rows = 4 inches/10cm in St st with larger needles
To save time, take time to check gauge.

Special Abbreviation

Inc (Increase): Knit into the front and back of st to inc 1 st.

Pattern Notes

The tote is worked in the rnd from the bottom up with the RS facing up to the flap.

The fold-down flap is worked with the WS facing, but will be folded down so that its RS will show.

Measurements are achieved using yarn and color specified; results may vary depending on yarn, yarn color and felting time.

Tote

Bottom

Cast on 64 sts. Join without twisting; place marker between first and last sts.

Rnd 1: Knit.

Rnd 2: *Inc, k1, inc, k26, inc, k1, inc; rep from * around. (72 sts)

Rnd 3: *K1, inc, k1, inc, k28, inc, k1, inc, k1; rep from * around. (80 sts)

Rnd 4: *K2, inc, k1, inc, k30, inc, k1, inc, k2; rep from * around. (88 sts)

Rnd 5: *K3, inc, k1, inc, k32, inc, k1, inc, k3; rep from * around. (96 sts)

Continued on page 53

Charming Button Bag

This cute little handbag is sure to become a favorite accessory for everyday use.

■■■□ INTERMEDIATE

Design by Donna Druchunas

Finished Felted Measurements

8 inches wide x 9 inches tall
Measurements are achieved using yarn and color specified; results may vary depending on yarn, yarn color and felting time.

Materials

- Plymouth Hand Paint Wool 100 percent wool super bulky weight yarn (60 yds/100g per skein): 3 skeins browns/tans #9
- Size 15 (10mm) 16-inch circular needle or size needed to obtain gauge
- Size N/P-15 (10mm) crochet hook, or size close to knitting-needle size
- Stitch marker
- Tapestry needle
- 2 (1⅛-inch) shank buttons
- Top-loading washing machine, zippered pillowcase, and laundry soap for felting

Pre-Felted Gauge

6 sts and 8 rows = 4 inches/10cm in St st using 2 strands of yarn held tog
Exact gauge is not critical; make sure your sts are loose and airy.

Pattern Notes

Bag is worked holding 2 strands of yarn tog throughout.

Bag

With circular needle and 2 strands of yarn held tog, cast on 32 sts. Join without twisting; place marker between first and last sts.

Knit every rnd until piece measures 9 inches from beg.
Bind off 16 sts. (16 sts)

Flap

Working back and forth on rem sts, knit every row until flap measures 3 inches.
Buttonhole row: K4, yo, k2tog, knit to last 6 sts, k2tog, yo, k4.
Next row: Knit.
Work even until flap measures 5 inches.
Bind off 1 st at beg of next 4 rows. (12 sts)
Bind off rem sts.

I-Cord Strap

Using 2 strands of yarn held tog, cast on 4 sts.
*K4, do not turn; sl sts back to LH needle; rep from * until cord is 12 inches.
Bind off.

Finishing

Sew handle onto top ridge of flap, approx 1½ inches from each edge.
Work 1 rnd of single crochet around flap and front opening of bag.
Weave in ends.

Felting

Felt following Felting instructions on page 172 until bag reaches finished measurements or desired size then gently rinse in the sink. Roll the bag in a towel and squeeze out the excess water.
Dry flat.
Sew buttons onto front of purse to correspond to buttonhole placement on flap. ❈

Chic Shrug

This soft and lovely lacy shrug will add a touch of warmth around the shoulders and arms.

■■□□ EASY

Design by Pauline Schultz

Sizes
Woman's small (medium, large) Instructions are given for smallest size, with larger sizes in parentheses. When only one number is given, it applies to all sizes.

Finished Measurements
Cuff to cuff: 50 (54, 58) inches
Back length: 12 (13½, 15) inches

Materials
- Plymouth Baby Alpaca Brush 80 percent baby alpaca/20 percent acrylic bulky weight yarn (110 yds/50g per ball): 3 (3, 4) balls mauve #567 (MC)
- Plymouth Tomorrow 40 percent nylon/38 percent mohair/18 percent acrylic/4 percent metal bulky weight yarn (82 yds/50g per ball): 1 (1, 2) balls rose multi #1663 (CC)
- Size 6 (4mm) 32-inch circular and double-pointed needles
- Size 9 (5.5mm) 32-inch circular needle or size needed to obtain gauge
- Size H/8 (5mm) crochet hook
- Tapestry needle

Gauge
18 sts and 22 rows = 4 inches/10cm in pat st with larger needle
To save time, take time to check gauge.

Special Technique
Crochet Cast On: Make a lp on the crochet hook. Hold needle horizontally behind hook and above lp. *Take yarn under needle and over front of hook. Pull yarn through. With 1 st on needle, bring yarn forward and rep from * for required number of sts. Last st is lp on hook—sl it to needle.

Pattern Stitch
Feather and Fan (multiple of 18 sts + 2)
Row 1: With CC, knit. Do not turn; slide sts to other end of needle.
Row 2: With MC, knit.
Row 3: With MC, k1, *[p2tog] 3 times, [yo, k1] 6 times, [p2tog] 3 times; rep from * to last st, k1.
Row 4: With MC, knit.
Row 5: With CC, purl. Do not turn; slide sts to other end of needle.
Row 6: With MC, purl.
Row 7: With MC, k1, *[k2tog] 3 times, [yo, k1] 6 times, [k2tog] 3 times; rep from * to last st, k1.
Row 8: With MC, purl.
Rep Rows 1–8 for pat.

Pattern Notes
Pat st is worked back and forth; a circular needle is used to accommodate the large number of sts and to allow knitter to slide sts from one end of needle to the other.

Shrug
Body
With smaller needle and MC, crochet cast on 164 (182, 200) sts.

Purl 6 rows.

With larger needle, work Rows 1–8 of Feather and Fan st 6 (7, 8) times; work Rows 1–5.

With smaller needle and MC, purl 5 rows.

Bind off loosely.

Cuff
With RS facing and smaller circular needle, pick up and knit 1 st in each garter ridge, 2 sts in each MC section of Feather and Fan, ending with 1 st in each garter ridge. (32, 36, 40 sts)

Distribute sts on dpns, join, and place marker between first and last sts.

Work in k1, p1 rib until cuff measures 6 inches.

Bind off loosely in pat.
Complete other cuff in the
same manner.

Finishing
Sew garter st edges tog for approx
3 inches above each cuff.
Weave in all ends.
Gently wash in lukewarm water and
dry flat. ❄

Wrap as You Wish Capelet

This lacy reversible wrap, with an easy stitch pattern that knits up quickly, will be stylishly warm during walks in the woods or on city streets.

 EASY

Design by Posey Salem

Finished Size
16 x 62 inches

Materials
- Plymouth Galway Worsted 100 percent wool medium weight yarn (210 yds/100g per ball): 5 balls bright green #145
- Size 6 (4.25mm) 24-inch circular needle
- Size 8 (5mm) 24-inch circular needle or size needed to obtain gauge
- 2 stitch markers
- Tapestry needle
- 1⅞-inch button
- Hook-and-eye closure (optional)
- Sewing needle and matching thread for button and hook (optional)

Gauge
18 sts and 27 rows = 4 inches/10cm in pat with larger needles (blocked)
To save time, take time to check gauge.

Pattern Stitch
Herringbone Lace Rib (multiple of 7 sts + 1)
Row 1 (RS): K1, *p1, k1, yo, p2tog, k1, p1, k1; rep from * to end.
Row 2: P1, *k2, yo, p2tog, k2, p1; rep from * to end.
Rep Rows 1 and 2 for pat.

Pattern Notes
Pattern is worked back and forth; a circular needle is used to accommodate the large number of sts.

The first st on every row is slipped purl-wise.

The yo between the knit st and the p2tog is wrapped forward and around the needle into purl position.

Capelet
Garter Stitch Edge
Using smaller needle, cast on 74 sts.
Slipping first st of every row, work in garter st for 1 inch, ending with a WS row.
Change to larger needles.

Body
Next row: Sl 1, k4, place marker, work Row 1 of Herringbone Lace Rib to last 5 sts, place marker, k5.
Continue in pats as established, slipping first st and working garter st edge before first and after last marker, until wrap measures 59½ inches from beg, ending with a WS row.

Buttonhole
Row 1: Sl 1, k4, work 41 sts in Herringbone Lace Rib; bind off 3 sts; beg with (yo, p2tog), continue in pats as established to end.
Row 2: Sl 1, k4, work in Herringbone Lace Rib to bound-off sts; cast on 3 sts; beg with (k1, yo, p2tog), continue in pats as established to end.
Row 3: Work in pats as established across, knitting 3 cast on sts tbl.
Work in pats as established for 10 rows, ending with a RS row.
Next row: Sl 1, k4, p1, *k2, p1, p1-tbl, k2, p1, rep from * to last 5 sts, end k5.

Garter Stitch Edge
Change to smaller needle.
Slipping first st of every row, work in

garter st for 1 inch, ending with a WS row.
Bind off all sts loosely.

Finishing
Weave in ends.
Block to finished measurements to open up the lace pattern.
Try on wrap and mark position for button so that wrap fits snugly. (If making wrap for a gift, mark button position measuring from side opposite buttonhole as follows: small: 40 inches, medium: 43 inches, large: 46 inches, extra-large: 49 inches, 2X-large: 52 inches.)
Sew on button.
Optional: Sew on hook-and-eye closure, with hook on upper corner above buttonhole and eye on upper edge positioned to connect with hook. ✻

Magical Möbius

Dropped stitches make a light and airy fabric. A twist before seaming creates the Möbius strip. Magic!

◼☐☐◻ BEGINNER

Design by Kristin Omdahl

Finished Size
22 x 44 inches (before seaming)

Materials
- Plymouth Yesterday 80 percent mohair/15 percent wool/5 percent nylon bulky weight yarn (110 yds/50g per ball): 3 balls brown multi #1703 (A)
- Plymouth Eros 100 percent nylon medium weight yarn (165 yds/50g per ball): 2 balls brown multi #7132 (B)
- Size 10.5 (6.5mm) straight needles or size needed to obtain gauge
- Tapestry needle

④ MEDIUM

⑤ BULKY

Gauge
12 sts and 12 rows = 4 inches/10cm garter st with A and B held tog
To save time, take time to check gauge.

Pattern Note
Möbius is worked holding 1 strand A and B held tog throughout.

Möbius
With A and B held tog, cast on 47 sts.
 Knit 140 rows. (70 garter ridges) [*Bind off 5 sts, cut yarn and pull through last st to fasten off*, re-attach yarn and k2] 6 times, work from * to *. Slide rem 12 sts off needles and gently drop sts down to cast-on edge.

Finishing
Weave in all ends.
 Gently wash the scarf in lukewarm water and dry flat to finished measurements.
 With the rectangle facing you, twist 1 side 180 degrees and pin both short edges tog, matching corners A and D, and B and C (see diagram).
 Sew the garter sections tog carefully and invisibly. ✳

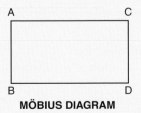

MÖBIUS DIAGRAM

Socks in All Sizes

These slipper socks are thick, cozy, and sized for just about anyone on your gift list. Make a pair for yourself or make a basketful for your guests to use.

■■■▢ INTERMEDIATE

Sizes

Toddler's (child's, adult's) Instructions are given for smallest size, with larger sizes in parentheses. When only 1 number is given, it applies to all sizes.

Finished Size

Foot length: Approx 6 (7, 10) inches

Materials

- Plymouth Encore Mega or Encore Colorspun Mega 75 percent acrylic/25 percent wool super bulky weight yarn (64 yds/100g per ball): 1 (1, 2) ball(s) orange #1316 (bright multi #7124, blue multi #7130)
- Size 11 (8mm) double-pointed needles (set of 4) or size needed to obtain gauge
- Stitch marker
- Tapestry needle

Gauge

10 sts and 14 rows = 4 inches/10cm in St st
To save time, take time to check gauge.

Special Abbreviation

MB (Make Bobble): [K1, p1] twice in same st (4 sts), then sl 2nd, 3rd, and 4th sts over the first st.

Pattern Stitch

Bobble Rib (even number of sts)
Rnd 1: *K1, p1; rep from * to end.
Rnd 2: *MB, p1; rep from * to end.
Rnds 3–11: *K1, p1; rep from * to end.

Pattern Note

These socks are loose and intended to fit a variety of foot sizes, e.g., the adult size can fit both a size 6 Woman's foot and a size 10 Men's. Adjust length as necessary.

Design by Christine L. Walter

Slipper Socks

Cuff

Cast on 14 (16, 20) sts. Distribute sts on 3 dpns as follows: 3-7-4 (4-8-4, 5-10-5).

Join without twisting; place marker between first and last sts.

Work Rnds 1–11 of Bobble Rib.

Divide for Heel

Next rnd: Work in rib as established across first needle, then transfer the sts from last needle to first needle for heel flap, leaving rem sts on hold on other needle for instep. (7, 8, 10 heel flap sts)

Heel Flap

Row 1 (WS): Sl 1 purlwise, purl across.
Row 2: Sl 1 knitwise, knit across.
  Rep [Rows 1 and 2] 1 (2, 3) time(s).
  Rep Row 1.

Turn heel

All sizes
Row 1 (RS): Sl 1, k2tog, k1 (2, 4), ssk, k1, turn.

Row 2: Sl 1, p4 (5, 7), turn.

Adult only
Row 3: Sl 1, k2tog, k2, ssk, k1, turn.
Row 4: Sl 1, p5, turn.

All sizes
Last row: K2tog, k1 (2, 2), ssk. (3, 4, 4 sts)

Gusset

With RS facing and using needle holding flap sts, pick up and knit 4 (5, 6) sts along left side of flap (Needle 1); with Needle 2, work in k1, p1 rib across instep, maintaining rib as established; with Needle 3, pick up and knit 4 (5, 6) sts along right side of flap, then knit 1 (2, 2) sts from Needle 1. Place marker for beg of rnd. There are 18 (22, 26) sts arranged 6-7-5 (7-8-7, 8-10-8).
Rnd 1: Needle 1: knit; Needle 2: work in rib as established; Needle 3: knit.
Rnd 2: Needle 1: Knit to last 2 sts, k2tog; Needle 2: rib as established; Needle 3: ssk, knit to end. (16, 20, 24 sts)

Child (Adult) only
Rep Rnds 1 and 2. (16, 18, 22 sts)

Foot

Work even in pat as established for 9 (12, 15) rows or until foot measures 1½ (1¾, 2) inches short of desired length.
Next rnd: Needle 1: knit to last 2 sts, k2tog; Needle 2: knit; Needle 3: ssk, knit to end. (14, 16, 20 sts)

Shape Toe

Rnd 1: Knit.
Rnd 2: Needle 1: knit to last 2 sts, k2tog; Needle 2: ssk, knit to last 2 sts, k2tog; Needle 3: ssk, knit to end. (10, 12, 16 sts)
  Rep [Rnds 1 and 2] 1 (1, 2) times. (6, 8, 8 sts)
  Knit to end of Needle 1.
  Cut yarn, leaving a 10-inch tail.

Graft Toe

Transfer sts from Needle 3 to Needle 1. (3, 4, 4 sts on each needle)
  Holding 2 needles parallel, weave toe referring to Kitchener Stitch instructions on page 173.

Finishing

Weave in ends. ❊

Not-Your-Basic Beanie
Continued from page 31

Shape Crown
Rnd 1: *K2, [LT] twice, CDD, [RT] twice, k3, rep from * around. (84 sts)
Rnd 2 and all even numbered rnds: Knit.
Rnd 3: *K3, LT, CDD, RT, k4, rep from * around. (72 sts)
Rnd 5: *K4, CDD, k5, rep from * around. (60 sts)
Rnd 7: *K3, CDD, k4, rep from * around. (48 sts)
Rnd 9: *K2, CDD, k3, rep from * around. (36 sts)

Rnd 11: *K1, CDD, k2, rep from * around. (24 sts)
Rnd 13: *CDD, k1, rep from * around. (12 sts)
Rnd 14: *Ssk, rep from * around. (6 sts)
Cut yarn, leaving a 6-inch tail.
  Using tapestry needle, thread tail through rem sts, and pull tight.

Finishing
Weave in ends.
  Block lightly. ❋

Fashionably Fringed Tote
Continued from page 40

Rnd 6: *K4, inc, k1, inc, k34, inc, k1, inc, k4; rep from * around. (104 sts)
Rnd 7: Purl.

Sides
Rnd 1: *K5, p1, k1, p1, k36, p1, k1, p1, k5, place marker; rep from * around.
  Work even in pat as established until piece measures 19 inches from beg.

Fringed Eyelet Flap
Rnds 1 and 2: *K1, p1; rep from * around.
Rnd 3: Knit.
  Purl around until flap measures 5 inches.
Next 3 rnds: *P1, k3; rep from * around.
Eyelet rnd: *P1, k2tog, yo, k1; rep from * around.
Next rnd: *K1, p3; rep from * around.
  Bind off very loosely purlwise.
  Fold flap down to show right side.

Fringe
Cut 26 (8-inch) strands of yarn. Referring to instructions on page 173, make Single Knot Fringe, using 1 strand for each knot; tie knots in each eyelet around flap. Trim even.

I-Cord Handles
Make 2
Leaving a 10-inch tail, cast on 4 sts.
  *K4, do not turn, sl sts back to LH needle; rep from * until cord is 30 inches long.
  Bind off.
  Cut yarn, leaving a 10-inch tail.

Finishing
Sew seam on bottom of bag.
  Lay tote flat and sew each end of a handle to inside of tote, positioned 6 inches from side folds and 1 inch down from flap fold. Rep on other side.

Felting
Tuck handles inside tote. Using cotton thread, baste top edge of tote closed.
  Felt following Felting Instructions on page 172 until tote reaches finished measurements or desired size then gently rinse in the sink. Roll the tote in a towel and squeeze out the excess water.
  Remove the cotton thread from opening.
  Stuff to shape (small boxes are good for shaping).
  Open up eyelet holes (if desired), and allow tote to air dry. ❋

The Stockings to Hang

Everyone in the family can have a unique knitted stocking. We have designs for assorted decor styles including traditional to bright modern styles—even big felted mittens for hanging on the mantel!

Razzle-Dazzle 'Em Stocking & Stars

"Razzle dazzle" your family with this nontraditional gold, magenta and purple stocking. Make extra stars for the tree!

◀■■■▷ INTERMEDIATE

Designs by Scarlet Taylor

Stocking

Finished Size
8 x 21 inches (excluding hanging loop)

Materials
• Plymouth Galway Worsted 100 percent wool medium weight yarn (210 yds/100g per ball): 1 ball magenta #141 (A) **[4 MEDIUM]**
• Plymouth Galway Chunky 100 percent wool bulky weight yarn (123 yds/100g per ball): 2 balls magenta #141 (B) **[5 BULKY]**
• Plymouth Stars 50 percent rayon/50 percent nylon medium weight yarn (71 yds/50g per ball): 2 balls purple #106 (C)
• Size 8 (5mm) straight needles
• Size 10 (6mm) straight and double-pointed knitting needles (set of 4) or size needed to obtain gauge
• 2 stitch markers
• Tapestry needle

Gauge
15 sts and 21 rows = 4 inches/10cm in St st with larger needles and B
To save time, take time to check gauge.

Special Abbreviations
N1, N2, N3: Needle 1, Needle 2, Needle 3
Ssp (slip, slip purl): Sl next 2 sts, one at a time as to knit, from LH needle to RH needle. Sl sts back onto LH needle keeping them twisted.
Purl these 2 sts tog tbl.

Pattern Notes
The cuff and legs are knit flat, then sts are divided to work heel; the gusset, foot and toe are worked in the round.
The cuff, heel, and toe are worked with 1 strand each of A and C held tog.

Stocking

Cuff
With smaller needles and 1 strand each of A and C held tog, cast on 62 sts.
Knit 3 rows.
Change to larger straight needles and work in St st until piece measures 2½ inches from beg, ending with a WS row.
Cut A and C.

Leg
With B, continue in St st until piece measures 11 inches from beg, ending with a RS row.
Next row (WS): Ssp, purl to last 2 sts, p2tog. (60 sts)
Cut B.

Heel
Divide sts among 3 dpns as follows: Sl 15 sts to each of 3 dpns. With 4th dpn and A and C held tog, knit rem 15 sts, then k15 from first dpn so that heel is joined. There are now 2 needles with 15 sts each (instep) and 1 needle with 30 sts (heel).
Work heel in St st for 2½ inches, ending with a WS row.

Heel Turn
Row 1 (RS): K17, ssk, k1, turn.
Row 2: Sl 1, p5, p2tog, p1, turn.
Row 3: Sl 1, k6, ssk, k1, turn.
Rows 4–12: Continue in this manner, working 1 more st before dec on each row. (18 sts)
Row 13: K9, place marker, k9.
Cut A and C.

Gusset
With RS facing, using same needle (now N1) and B, pick up and knit 10 sts along side of heel flap; with N2, knit 30 instep sts; with N3, pick up and knit 10 sts along other side of heel flap, then k9 to marker. (68 sts arranged N1: 19 sts; N2: 30 sts; N3: 19 sts)
Knit 1 rnd.
Dec rnd: N1: knit to last 3 sts, k2tog, k1; N2: knit; N3: k1, ssk, knit to end of rnd. (66 sts)
Continue in St st and rep Dec rnd [every 3rd rnd] 3 times. (60 sts)

Foot
Work even until foot measures approx 7½ inches from beg of heel turn.
Cut B.

Toe

Work with 1 strand each of A and C held tog.

Dec rnd: N1: knit to last 3 sts, k2tog, k1; N2: k1, ssk, knit to last 3 sts, k2tog, k1; N3: k1, ssk, knit to end. (56 sts)

Rep Dec rnd [every other rnd] 3 times, then [every rnd] 6 times. (20 sts)

With N3, k5 sts on N1. (10 sts each needle)

Cut yarn, leaving a 16-inch tail.

Finishing

Graft toe tog with Kitchener st. (see page 173)

Weave in all ends.

Sew back leg seam.
Block.

Hanging Loop

With B, cast on 4 sts.

*K4, do not turn, sl sts back to LH needle; rep from * until loop is 2½ inches.

Bind off.

Sew ends tog, then attach to inside of stocking at back seam.

Embellish with Felted Stars.

Felted Stars

Materials

- Plymouth Galway Worsted 100 percent wool medium weight yarn (210 yds/100g per ball): 1 ball each dark apricot #154 (A) and light apricot #137 (B)
- Size 11 (8mm) straight needles
- Clear-drying fabric glue
- Crystal glitter
- Approx 6 yds ³⁄₁₆-inch-wide ribbon

Pre-Felted Gauge

13 sts and 17 rows = 4 inches/10cm
in St st

Exact gauge is not critical; make sure
your sts are loose and airy.

Star

*Pattern Note: Yarn amount is sufficient to
make stars for stocking, ornaments and
tree skirt on page 110.*

*With A, cast on 40 sts.

Work in St st until piece measures
approx 12½ inches.

Bind off.

Rep from * until you have enough for
the stars you desire.

With B, work squares as for A.

Weave in yarn ends.

Follow basic felting instructions on
page 172 until you can no longer see
the st definition.

Lay flat to dry.

Use star templates to trace and cut
out number of stars desired.

Decorate with glitter.

Glue stars to stocking as desired.

For ornaments, use tapestry needle
to thread ribbon through point of star.
Tie ribbon to hang. ❋

For coordinating Razzle-Dazzle Tree Skirt, see page 110.

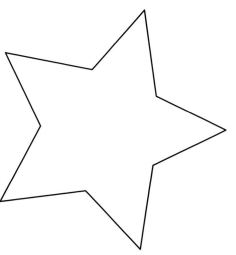

STAR TEMPLATES

Don't Open 'til December 25

Tie ribbons around the presents and trim the tree—let your imagination be your guide.

■■■□ INTERMEDIATE

Design by Sara Louise Harper

Finished Size

Approx 7¾ x 22 inches (excluding hanging loop)

Materials

- Plymouth Country 8 Ply 100 percent superwash wool medium weight yarn (105 yards/50g per ball): 2 balls cream #2234 (A); 1 ball each pine green #2276 (B), Christmas red #2232 (C), gray #216 (D), gold #2269 (E), leaf green #2250 (F) and yellow #1085 (G)
- Size 7 (4.5mm) straight and double-pointed needles (set of 4) or size needed to obtain gauge
- Tapestry needle
- Multicolored beads (for embellishment, optional)

Gauge

19 sts and 26 rows = 4 inches/10cm in St st
To save time, take time to check gauge.

Special Abbreviations

N1, N2, N3: Needle 1, Needle 2, Needle 3

Pattern Stitch

K2, P2 Rib
Row 1 (RS): K2, *p2, k2; rep from * across.
Row 2: P2, *k2, p2; rep from * across.
Rep Rows 1 and 2 for pat.

Pattern Notes

The leg is knit flat in rows, then divided to work heel; the gusset, foot and toe are worked in the round.

The first and last sts of leg are selvage sts and are worked in St st; they will be eliminated before working the heel. Work all dec within these sts.

"NOEL" in Chart B may be replaced by a name if desired.

Stocking

With straight needles and B, cast on 66 sts.
Work 4 rows in K2, P2 Rib.
Work 8 rows of Chart A.
Work 9 rows of Chart B.
With B, work 2 rows in St st.
Work 51 rows of Chart C; dec 1 st each side on rows 4, 16 and 26 as shown on chart. (60 sts)
With A, work 6 rows in St st.
With B, knit 1 row.
Next row (WS): P2tog, purl to last 2 sts, ssp. (58 sts)
Cut B.

Heel

Divide sts among 3 dpns as follows: Sl 14 sts to N1, 15 sts to N2 and 14 sts to N3. With 4th dpn and A and C, work Row 3 of Chart A across rem 15 sts, then continue in pat across the 14 sts on the first needle (heel is joined). There are now 2 needles with 29 sts divided between them (instep) and 1 needle with 29 sts (heel).
Next row: Working on heel sts only,

work Row 4 of Chart A.
Continue in color pat as established for 3 inches, ending with a RS row.

Heel Turn

Maintaining color pat as established, turn heel as follows:
Row 1 (WS): Sl 1, p14, p2tog, p1, turn.
Row 2: Sl 1, k2, ssk, k1, turn.
Row 3: Sl 1, p3, p2tog, p1, turn.
Rows 4–12: Continue in this manner, working 1 more st before dec on each row.
Row 13: Sl 1, p13, p2tog, turn. Cut C.
Row 14: With A only, k14, ssk. Do not turn. (15 sts)

Gusset

With RS facing, using same needle (now N1), pick up and knit 15 sts along side of heel flap; N2: knit 29 instep sts; N3: pick up and knit 15 sts along other side of heel flap, then k7 from N1. (74 sts arranged N1: 22 sts, N2: 29 sts, N3: 23 sts)
Dec rnd: N1: knit to last 3 sts, k2tog, k1; N2: knit; N3: k1, ssk, knit to end. (72 sts)
Continue in St st, rep Dec rnd [every other rnd] 7 times. (58 sts)
Knit until foot measures 7 inches from back of heel.
Change to B and knit 4 rnds.

Toe

Dec rnd: N1: knit to last 3 sts, k2tog, k1; N2: k1, ssk, knit to last 3 sts, k2tog, k1; N3: k1, ssk, knit to end. (54 sts)
Continue in St st, rep Dec rnd [every

other rnd] 6 times, then [every rnd] 3 times. (18 sts)

With N3, knit all sts on N1. (9 sts each needle)

Cut yarn, leaving a 16-inch tail.

Finishing

Graft toe tog with Kitchener st (see page 173).

Weave in all ends.

Sew back leg seam.
Block.

Embellishments

Decorate tree and packages following photo (or as desired) using lengths of yarn or beads.

Hanging Loop

With A, cast on 3 sts.

*K3, do not turn, sl sts back to LH needle; rep from * for approx 7 inches.

Bind off.

Sew ends tog, then attach to inside of stocking at back seam. ✹

COLOR KEY
- ☐ Cream (A)
- ■ Pine green (B)
- ■ Christmas red (C)
- ■ Gray (D)
- ■ Gold (E)
- ■ Leaf green (F)
- ■ Yellow (G)

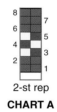

CHART A

2-st rep

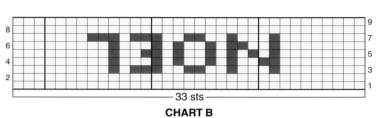

— 33 sts —

CHART B

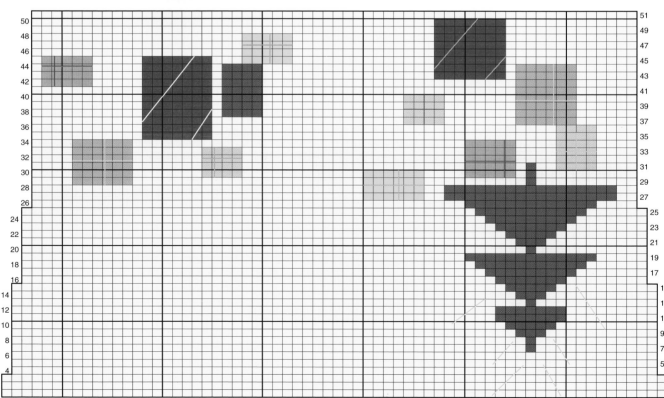

CHART C

Sweet Surprises

Only Santa will know what wonderful treats are inside this stocking!

Finished Size
Approx 6½ x 23 inches (excluding hanging lp)

Materials
- Plymouth Encore Worsted 75 percent acrylic/25 percent wool medium weight yarn (200 yds/100g per ball): 1 ball each natural #146 (MC) and red #9601 (CC)
- Size 8 (5mm) straight and double-pointed needles (set of 4) or size needed to obtain gauge
- Stitch marker
- Tapestry needle

Gauge
20 sts and 26 rows = 4 inches/10cm in St st
To save time, take time to check gauge.

Special Abbreviations
MB (Make Bobble): [K1, p1, k1, p1, k1] into st, turn; p5, turn; k5, turn; p5, turn; k5, pass first 4 sts over last st.
N1, N2, N3: Needle 1, Needle 2, Needle 3
Ssp (Slip, slip, purl): Sl next 2 sts, one at a time as to knit, from LH to RH needle. Sl these sts back onto LH needle keeping them twisted. Purl 2 sts tog-tbl.

Pattern Stitch
Lace Rib (multiple of 6 sts + 2)
Rows 1 and 3 (WS): P1 (edge st), *k1, p5; rep from * to last st, p1 (edge st).
Row 2: K1, *k2tog, yo, k1, yo, ssk, p1; rep from * to last st, k1.

Design by Celeste Pinheiro

Row 4: K1, *k5, p1; rep from * to last st, k1.
Rep Rows 1–4 for pat.

Pattern Notes
The leg is knit in rows, then divided to work heel; the gusset, foot and toe are worked in the round.

The first and last sts of leg are selvage sts and are worked in St st; they will be eliminated before working the heel.

Stocking
Cuff
With MC, cast on 62 sts.
Work 16 rows in Lace Rib.

Leg
Knit 1 WS row.
Eyelet row (RS): K1, *k2tog, yo; rep from * to last st, k1.
Knit 1 WS row.
Work 2 rows in St st.
Bobble row (RS): K4, *MB, k5; rep from * to last 4 sts, MB, k3.
Work 13 rows in St st.
Rep Eyelet row.
Knit 1 WS row.
Work 4 rows in rev St st.
Maintaining first and last sts in St st, work 2 reps of chart across center 60 sts.
Work 4 rows in rev St st.
Rep Eyelet row.
Work 3 rows in St st.
Rep Bobble row.
Work 2 rows in St st.
Next row: Ssp, purl to last 2 sts, p2tog. (60 sts)
Cut yarn.

Heel
Divide sts among 3 dpns as follows: Sl 15 sts to each of 3 dpns. With 4th dpn and MC, knit rem 15 sts, then k15 from first dpn so that heel is joined. There are now 2 needles with 15 sts each (instep) and 1 needle with 30 sts (heel).
Work in St st for 13 rows, ending with a WS row.

Heel Turn
Row 1 (RS): K16, ssk, turn.
Row 2: Sl 1, p3, p2tog, p1, turn.
Row 3: Sl 1, k4, ssk, k1, turn.
Rows 4–12: Continue in this manner, working 1 more st before dec on each row.
Row 13: Sl 1, k14, ssk, turn.
Row 14: P15, p2tog, turn. (16 sts)
Row 15: K8, place marker, k8.

Gusset

With RS facing and using same needle (now N1), pick up and knit 11 sts along side of heel flap; with N2, knit 30 instep sts; with N3, pick up and knit 11 sts along edge of rem heel flap, then k8 to marker. Join. (68 sts arranged N1: 19 sts; N2: 30 sts; N3: 19 sts)

Dec rnd: N1: knit to last 2 sts, k2tog, k1; N2: knit; N3: k1, ssk, knit to end of rnd. (66 sts)

Continue in St st and rep Dec rnd [every 3rd rnd] 3 times. (60 sts)

Knit 1 rnd.

Foot

Rnd 1: Purl.
Rnd 2: *K2tog, yo; rep from * around.
Rnd 3: Purl.
Rnds 4–9: Knit.

Rep [Rnds 1–9] twice.

Toe

Dec rnd: *N1: knit to last 3 sts, k2tog, k1; N2: k1, ssk knit to last 3 sts, k2tog, k1; N3: k1, ssk, knit to end. (56 sts)

Rep Dec rnd [every other rnd] 3 times, then [every rnd] 6 times. (20 sts)

With N3, knit 5 sts on N1. (10 sts each needle)

Cut yarn, leaving a 16-inch tail.

Finishing

Graft toe tog with Kitchener st (see page 173).

Sew back leg seam.

I-Cord Heart

With MC, make 4 I-cords as follows:

Cast on 4 sts.

*K4, do not turn, sl sts back to LH needle; rep from * for approx 7 inches.

Bind off.

Sew down around heart shape as in photo.

Embroidery

With CC, embroider as desired, or as in photo as follows:

Over cast along cast-on edge.

With chain st, embroider name between first row of bobbles and Heart pat.

Run CC under every other st on row between Lace Rib and Eyelet row.

Embroider flowers using Lazy Daisy sts inside and around Heart.

Run CC under every other st between last 2 purl rows below Heart.

Work cross-sts below last row of bobbles.

Hanging Loop

Cut 4 strands CC and 2 strands MC 15 inches long.

Knot at 1 end, leaving 1½-inch tails.

Divide yarn into 2 groups (each 2 CC and 1 MC), make 3-strand braid.

Knot end, leaving 1½-inch tails.

Fold in half and attach center to stocking at back seam.

Make an overhand knot forming a loop approx 3 inches long. ✳

LAZY-DAISY STITCH

CHAIN STITCH

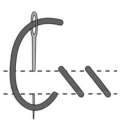

CROSS-STITCH

STITCH KEY
☐ K on WS, p on WS
⊟ P on RS, k on WS

SWEET SURPRISES
— 30-st panel —

Felted Mittens

Here's a novel idea—hang mittens for Santa to fill, instead of stockings.

Design by Anita Closic

Finished Felted Measurements

Approx 5½ x 10 inches (excluding hanging loop)

Materials

- Plymouth Galway Worsted 100 percent wool medium weight yarn (210 yds/100g per ball): [colorway 1] 1 ball each pink #141 (A), orange #91 (B) and gold #137 (C); [colorway 2] 1 ball each turquoise #149 (A), blue #129 (B) and purple #153 (C)
- Plymouth Hot! Hot! Hot! 65 percent nylon/30 percent polyester/5 percent acrylic super bulky weight yarn (33 yds/50g per ball): 1 ball for each mitten multicolor #692 (D)
- Size 13 (9mm) straight needles
- 2 stitch markers
- 2 stitch holders
- Tapestry needle

Pre-Felted Gauge

10 sts and 13 rows = 4 inches/10cm with 2 strands held tog

Exact gauge is not critical; make sure your sts are loose and airy.

The Finished Felted Measurements were achieved using yarns and colors specified. Results may vary depending on yarn, yarn color and felting time.

Special Abbreviation

Inc (Increase): Inc 1 by knitting in front and back of st.

Pattern Note

Mitten is worked holding 2 strands yarn held tog throughout, except cuff.

Mitten

Cuff

With 2 strands A and 1 strand D held tog, cast on 36 sts.

Work in garter st for 3½ inches, ending with a WS row. Cut D.

With 2 strands A, work 6 rows in St st, placing a marker on either side of center 2 sts on last row.

Thumb Gusset

Inc row (RS): Knit to marker, sl marker, inc, knit to next marker, inc, sl marker, knit to end. (38 sts)

Next row: Purl.

Continued on page 77

Cool Snowman & Santa Stockings

This snowman won't melt, even when hanging by the fireplace!
HO, HO, HO! This Santa stocking will hold lots of goodies!

Designs by Scarlet Taylor

Cool Snowman

Finished Size
Approx 9 x 21 inches (excluding hanging loop)

Materials
- Plymouth Galway Worsted 100 percent wool medium weight yarn (210 yds/100g per ball): 2 balls green #82 (A); 1 ball each red #150 (B), off-white #1 (C), black #9 (D) and blue #129 (E)
- Size 8 (5mm) straight and double-pointed needles (set of 4) or size needed to obtain gauge
- Size 6/0 seed beads: 3 each pink and blue
- 2 stitch markers
- Sharp sewing needle
- White thread
- Tapestry needle
- 2 snowflake buttons
- White mini pompom

Gauge
20 sts and 26 rows = 4 inches/10cm in St st
To save time, take time to check gauge.

Special Abbreviations
N1, N2, N3: Needle 1, Needle 2, Needle 3
Ssp (slip, slip, purl): Sl next 2 sts, one at a time as if to knit, from LH needle to RH needle. Sl sts back onto LH needle keeping them twisted. Purl these 2 sts tog tbl.

Pattern Notes
When working Border pat (Chart A), use Fair Isle technique, stranding color not in use on WS.

When working Snowman motif (Chart B), use intarsia technique, using separate lengths of yarn for each colored section; bring new color up from under old color to lock them.

The leg is knit flat in rows, then divided to work heel; the gusset, foot

and toe are worked in the round.

The first and last sts of leg are selvage sts and are worked in St st; they will be eliminated before working the heel.

Snowman Stocking
Hem
With straight needles and A, cast on 94 sts.

Work 16 rows in St st, beg with a RS row.
Next row (RS): Purl across for hem turning ridge.

Border
Next row: Purl.
Work Chart A. Cut B.
With A, work 3 rows in St st.

Leg
Set-up row (RS): K50, place marker, work Row 1 of Chart B across next 38 sts, place marker, k6.

Continue in St st in pats as established, until Chart B is complete.
Cut all yarns but A.
Work 6 rows in St st.
Next row (WS): P2tog, purl to last 2 sts, ssp. (92 sts)
Cut A.

Heel Flap
Divide sts among 3 dpns as follows: Sl 23 sts to each of 3 dpns. With 4th dpn and B, knit rem 23 sts, then k23 from first dpn so that heel is joined. There

are now 2 needles with 23 sts each (instep) and 1 needle with 46 sts (heel).

Work heel in St st for 2½ inches, ending with a WS row.

Heel Turn

Row 1 (RS): K25, ssk, k1, turn.
Row 2: Sl 1, p5, p2tog, p1, turn.
Row 3: Sl 1, k6, ssk, k1, turn.
Rows 4–20: Continue in this manner, working 1 more st before dec on each row. (26 sts)
Row 21: K13, place marker, k13. Cut B.

Gusset

With RS facing and using same needle (now N1) and A, pick up and knit 13 sts along side of heel flap; with N2, knit 46 instep sts; with N3, pick up and knit 13 sts along other edge of heel flap, then k13 to marker. (98 sts arranged N1: 26 sts; N2: 46 sts; N3: 26 sts)

Knit 1 rnd.
Dec rnd: N1: knit to last 3 sts, k2tog, k1; N2: knit; N3: k1, ssk, knit to end of rnd. (96 sts)

Continue in St st and Dec rnd [every 3rd rnd] twice. (92 sts)

Foot

Work even until foot measures approx 7½ inches from back of heel.

Cut A and join B.

Toe

Dec rnd: *N1: knit to last 3 sts, k2tog, k1; N2: k1, ssk, knit to last 3 sts, k2tog, k1; N3: k1, ssk, knit to end. (88 sts)

[Rep Dec rnd] 17 times. (20 sts)

With N3, knit 5 sts on N1. (10 sts each needle)

Cut yarn, leaving a 16-inch tail.

Finishing

Graft toe tog with Kitchener st (see page 173).

Weave in all ends.

Sew back leg seam.

Fold hem to inside of stocking at turning ridge and sew in place.

Embellishments

Note: Refer to embroidery st illustrations on page 69.

Embroider black French knots for Snowman's eyes.

Embroider a basic outline stitch in black for brows, and mouth.

Embroider 2 black elongated French knots for nose, wrapping yarn around needle 6 times.

Attach white pompom to end of hat. Sew snowflake buttons to snowman's sweater.

Sew 1 seed bead at center of each snowflake around snowman.

COLOR KEY
- ■ Green (A)
- ■ Red (B)
- □ Off-white (C)
- ■ Black (D)
- ■ Blue (E)

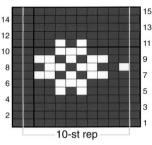

SNOWMAN CHART A

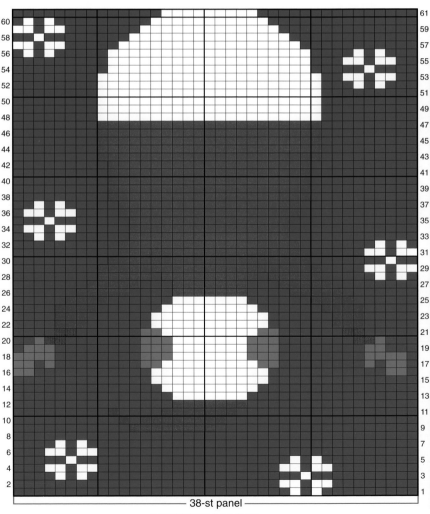

10-st rep

38-st panel

SNOWMAN CHART B

Snowman's Scarf I-Cords

Make 2

With E, cast on 4 sts.

*K4, do not turn, sl sts back to LH needle; rep from * for approx 2¼ inches.

Bind off.

Cut 6 strands of white yarn, 2 inches long. Attach 3 strands to 1 end of each I-cord for "fringe."

Trim even to desired length.

Refer to photo for scarf placement and sew I-cords in place.

Hanging Loop

With A, cast on 3 sts.

I-cord: *K3, do not turn, sl sts back to LH needle; rep from * for approx 2½ inches.

Bind off.

Sew ends tog, then attach to inside of stocking at back seam. ❈

Santa Stocking

Finished Size

Approx 8½ x 21 inches (excluding hanging loop)

Materials

- Plymouth Galway Worsted  100 percent wool medium weight yarn (210 yds/100g per ball): 2 balls green #82 (A); 1 ball each red #150 (B), off-white #1 (C), black #9 (D) and pink #135 (E)
- Size 8 (5mm) straight and double-pointed needles (set of 4) or size needed to obtain gauge
- Small amount of blue and white embroidery floss
- 2 present-shaped buttons
- 2 stitch markers
- Tapestry needle

Gauge

20 sts and 26 rows = 4 inches/10cm in St st

To save time, take time to check gauge.

Special Abbreviations

N1, N2, N3: Needle 1, Needle 2, Needle 3

Pattern Notes

When working Border pat (Chart A), use Fair Isle technique, stranding color not in use on WS.

When working Santa motif (Chart B), use intarsia technique, using separate lengths of yarn for each colored section; bring new color up from under old color to lock them.

The leg is knit flat in rows, then divided to work heel; the gusset, foot and toe are worked in rnds.

The first and last sts of leg are selvage sts and are worked in St st; they will be eliminated before working the heel.

Stocking

Hem

With straight needles and A, cast on 82 sts. Work 16 rows in St st, beg with a RS row.
Next row (RS): Purl across for hem turning ridge.

Border

Next row: Purl.
Join B, and work Chart A. Cut B.
With A, work 3 rows in St st.

Leg

Set-up row (RS): K47, place marker, work Row 1 of Chart B across next 28 sts, place marker, k7.
Continue in St st in pats as established until Chart B is complete.
Cut all yarns but A.
Work 3 rows even in St st.
Next row (WS): P2tog, purl to last 2 sts, ssp. (80 sts)
Cut A.

Heel Flap

Divide sts among 3 dpns as follows: Sl 20 sts to each of 3 dpns. With 4th dpn and B, knit rem 20 sts, then k20 from first dpn so that heel is joined. There

are now 2 needles with 20 sts each (instep) and 1 needle with 40 sts (heel).

Work heel in St st for 2½ inches, ending with a WS row.

Heel Turn

Row 1 (RS): Sl 1, k21, ssk, k1, turn.
Row 2: Sl 1, p5, p2tog, p1, turn.
Row 3: Sl 1, k6, ssk, k1, turn.

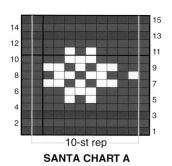

SANTA CHART A

COLOR KEY
- Green (A)
- Red (B)
- Off-white (C)
- Black (D)
- Pink (E)
- • Blue French knot

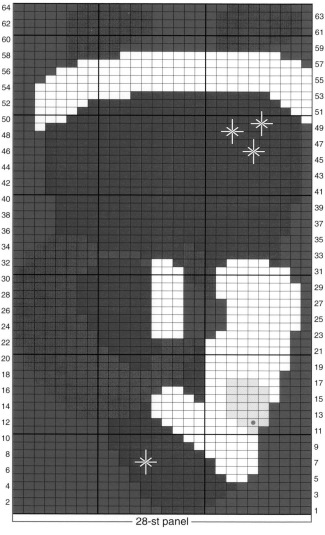

SANTA CHART B

Rows 4–16: Continue in this manner, working 1 more st before dec on each row.
Row 17: Sl 1, k20, ssk, turn.
Row 18: Sl 1, p20, p2tog, turn. (22 sts)
Row 19: K11, place marker, k11. Cut B.

Gusset

With RS facing and using same needle (now N1) and A, pick up and knit 14 sts along side of heel flap; with N2, knit 40 instep sts; with N3, pick up and knit 14 sts along other side of heel flap, then k11 to marker. Join. (90 sts arranged N1: 25 sts; N2: 40 sts; N3: 25 sts)
   Knit 1 rnd.
Dec rnd: N1: knit to last 3 sts, k2tog, k1; N2: knit; N3: k1, ssk, knit to end of rnd. (88 sts)
   Continue in St st rep Dec rnd [every 3rd rnd] 4 times. (80 sts)

Foot

Work even until foot measures approx 7½ inches from back of heel.
   Cut A and join B.

Toe

Dec rnd: N1: knit to last 3 sts, k2tog, k1; N2: k1, ssk, knit to last 3 sts, k2tog, k1; N3: k1, ssk, knit to end. (76 sts)
   Rep Dec rnd 14 times. (20 sts)
With N3, k5 sts on N1. (10 sts each needle)
   Cut yarn, leaving a 16-inch tail.

Finishing

Graft toe tog with Kitchener st (see page 173).
   Weave in all ends.
   Sew back leg seam.
   Fold hem to inside of stocking at turning ridge and sew in place.
   Block.

Embellishments

Refer to Chart B for eye and snowflake placement.
   With blue floss, embroider 1 French knot for Santa's eye.

With white floss, embroider stars for snowflakes on Santa's coat and hat (see Chart C).
   Sew buttons to top of Santa's bag.

Hanging Loop

With A, cast on 3 sts.
   *K3, do not turn, sl sts back to LH needle; rep from * for approx 2½ inches.
   Bind off.
   Sew ends tog, then attach to inside of stocking at back seam. ❋

FRENCH KNOT

CHART C

OUTLINE STITCH

Holly Stocking Duo

Knit in the round, these children's-sized, holly-embellished stockings will work up quickly.

◖■■▢ INTERMEDIATE

Designs by Debbie O'Neill

Sizes
Baby (Child) Instructions are given for smaller size, with larger size in parentheses. When only 1 number is given, it applies to both sizes.

Finished Measurements
5½ (6½) inches wide x 12 (15) inches long

Materials
- Plymouth Galway Worsted 100 percent wool medium weight yarn (210 yds/100g per ball): 2 balls red #44 (MC); 1 ball each off-white #1 (A) and green #82 (B)
- Size 5 (3.75mm) 16-inch circular and double-pointed needles (set of 4) or size needed to obtain gauge
- 6 inches ⅞-inch-wide green grosgrain ribbon per stocking
- Green sewing thread
- Tapestry needle
- Sharp sewing needle
- Stitch markers

Gauge
22 sts and 31 rnds = 4 inches/10cm in St st
To save time, take time to check gauge.

Special Abbreviations
RT (Right Twist): Knit 2nd st on LH needle and leave resulting st on LH needle; knit first st on LH needle, then sl both sts to RH needle.
N1, N2, N3: Needle 1, Needle 2, Needle 3

Pattern Stitches
A. Baby Cable Rib (multiple of 4 sts)
Rnds 1, 3, and 4: *K2, p2; rep from * around.
Rnd 2: *RT, p2; rep from * around.
Rep Rnds 1–4 for pat.
B. Dot St (multiple of 4 sts)
Rnds 1, 2, and 4: Knit.
Rnd 3: *K2, p1, k1; rep from * around.
Rnds 5, 6, and 8: Knit.
Rnd 7: *P1, k3; rep from * around.
Rep Rnds 1–8 for pat.

Pattern Note
Materials given are sufficient for both stockings; if making only 1 stocking, use 1 ball each MC, A and B.

Stocking
Leg
With circular needle and MC, cast on 64 (72) sts. Join without twisting; place marker between first and last sts for beg of rnd.

Work 3 or 4 reps of Baby Cable Rib, as desired. (The baby stocking is shown with 4 reps; the child's stocking is shown with 3 reps.)

Work 3 rnds St st. Cut MC.

Work Rnds 1–14 of chart: [Baby size only: Dec 1 st on first rnd. (63 sts)]

Increase 1 st on last rnd. (64 sts)

Cut A and B.

With MC, work Dot St until piece measures 8 (10½) inches from beg. Cut MC.

Heel Flap
With either A or B (as desired), knit

16 (18) sts from circular needle onto a dpn; turn.

Sl 1, p31 (33) sts. These 32 (36) sts are the heel sts; keep the rem 32 (36) sts on hold on the circular needle for instep.

Work back and forth on heel sts only.
Row 1: *Sl 1, k1; rep from * to end of row.

Row 2: Sl 1, purl to end of row.

Rep [Rows 1 and 2] 15 (17) times.

Heel Turn

Row 1: K18 (20), ssk, k1, turn.

Row 2: Sl 1, p5, p2tog, p1, turn.

Row 3: Sl 1, k6, ssk, k1, turn.

Rows 4–12 (14): Continue in this manner, working 1 more st before dec on each row.

Row 13 (15): Sl 1, knit to last 2 sts, ssk.

Row 14 (16): Sl 1, purl to last 2 sts, p2tog. (18, 20 sts rem)

Cut A or B.

Row 15 (17): With MC, K9 (10), place marker, k9 (10).

Gusset

With RS facing and using same needle (now N1), pick up and knit 16 (18) sts along side of heel flap; with N2, knit 32 (36) instep sts in Dot St as established; with N3, pick up and knit 16 (18) sts along other edge of heel flap, then knit to marker. Join. [82 (92) sts arranged N1: 25 (28) sts; N2: 32 (36) sts; N3: 25 (28) sts]

Knit 1 rnd.

Dec rnd: N1: knit to last 3 sts, k2tog, k1; N2: work in Dot St; N3: k1, ssk, knit to end of rnd. (80, 90 sts)

Continue working sts on N1 and N3 in St st and sts on N2 in Dot St, rep Dec rnd [every other rnd] 8 (9) times. (64, 72 sts)

Foot

Work even in pats as established until foot measures 6 (6½) inches from back of heel. Cut MC.

Toe

With either A or B as desired, knit 1 rnd.

Dec rnd: N1: knit to last 3 sts, k2tog, k1; N2: k1, ssk, knit to last 3 sts, k2tog, k1; N3: k1, ssk, knit to end. (60, 68 sts)

Continue in St st, rep Dec rnd [every other rnd] 10 (12) times. (20 sts)

With N3, knit 5 sts on N1. (10 sts each needle)

Cut yarn, leaving a 16-inch tail.

Finishing

Graft toe tog with Kitchener st (see page 173).

Weave in all ends.

Holly Berry Bobbles

Make as many as desired

Leaving a 5-inch tail, cast on 1 st.

Row 1: [K1, yo, k1, yo, k1] into the st. (5 sts)

Row 2: Purl.

Row 3: Knit.

Row 4: P2tog, k1, p2tog. (3 sts)

Row 5: Sl 1, k2tog, psso. (1 st)

Cut yarn, leaving a 5-inch tail.

Fasten off.

Sew bobbles to leaf area as desired (see photo).

Gently wash in cold water; block and allow to dry.

When dry, use sewing thread and needle to attach the grosgrain ribbon to the cuff as a hanging loop. ❄

HOLLY STOCKING DUO

9-st rep

14 13 12 11 10 9 8 7 6 5 4 3 2 1

COLOR KEY
☐ Off-white (A)
■ Green (B)

Felted Mittens

Continued from page 66

Rep [last 2 rows] twice. (42 sts)

Cut 1 strand A and attach 1 strand B.

With A and B held tog, rep [last 2 rows] 4 times. (50 sts, 16 sts between markers)

Thumb

Cut A and attach 2nd strand B.

Next row: With 2 strands B held tog, k17 and sl to holder, k16, sl rem 17 sts to holder.

Work 5 rows in St st.

Dec row: Ssk, knit to last 2 sts, k2tog. (14 sts)

Next row: Purl.

Rep last 2 rows. (12 sts)

Cut yarn, leaving an 8-inch tail.

Using tapestry needle, thread tail through rem sts and pull tight. Secure end.

Hand

With RS facing and 2 strands B held tog, knit 17 sts on 2nd holder.

Next row: P17, p17 from first holder. (34 sts)

Work 5 rows in St st.

Cut 1 strand B, and attach 1 strand C.

With B and C held tog, work 4 rows in St st.

Cut B, and attach 2nd strand C.

With 2 strands C held tog, work 4 rows in St st.

Top

Row 1 (RS): K4, *k2tog, k3; rep from * across. (28 sts)

Rows 2 and 4: Purl.

Row 3: * K1, k2tog, k1; rep from * across. (21 sts)

Row 4: Purl

Row 5: *K1, k2tog; rep from * across row. (14 sts)

Row 6: P2tog across. (7 sts)

Cut yarn, leaving a 12-inch tail.

Using tapestry needle, thread tail through rem sts, and pull tight. Secure end.

Finishing

Weave in all ends.

Sew side and thumb seams.

Hanging Loop

With 2 strands A held tog, cast on 4 sts.

*K4, do not turn, sl sts back to LH needle; rep from * for 14 inches.

Bind off.

Attach both ends to top of mitten, forming loop.

Felting

Follow basic felting instructions on page 172 until finished measurements are obtained or mitten is desired size.

Shape and dry flat. ❄

Deck the Halls, Trim the Trees

Here are decorations to create a wondrous holiday look around your house. We've included tree trimmings, gift wrappings and festive additions for your dining table and mantel.

Felted Pot Cozies

Decorate your home with these festive, felted flowerpot covers, filling them with candies, potpourri or little Christmas trees.

◼️◼️◻️◻️ EASY

Design by Christine L. Walter

Size
Fits average 5-inch flowerpot

Finished Felted Measurement
Approx 4 inches tall

Materials
- Plymouth Galway Worsted 100 percent wool medium weight yarn (210 yds/100g per ball): 1 ball light aqua #111, light green #146 or fuchsia #141 (MC)

  4 MEDIUM
- Plymouth Stars 50 percent rayon/50 percent nylon medium weight yarn (71 yds/50g per ball): 1 ball white #102 (CC)
- Size 10½ (6.5mm) double-pointed needles or size needed to obtain gauge
- 8 stitch markers (1 in CC for beg of rnd)
- Tapestry needle
- 5-inch flowerpot for each cozy

Pre-Felted Gauge
15 sts and 21 rows = 4 inches/10cm in St st with 1 strand MC
Exact gauge is not critical; make sure your sts are loose and airy.

Pattern Notes
Cozy is knit in the round from the top down.

1 ball MC will make 1 cozy.

Finished Felted Measurement is achieved using yarns and colors specified; results may vary depending on yarn, yarn color and felting time.

Pot Cozy
Sides
With 1 strand of CC, cast on 64 sts and distribute on 3 dpns.

Join without twisting; place marker between first and last sts.

Join 1 strand MC (in color of choice) at beg of next rnd and work with strand of CC and MC held tog.

Rnd 1: Knit.

Rnd 2: Purl.

Rnd 3: Knit.

Cut CC and continue with MC only.

Knit 14 rnds.

Next rnd: *K8, place marker; rep from * around.

Bottom
Dec rnd: *Knit to 2 sts before marker, k2tog; rep from * around. (56 sts)

Continue in St st rep Dec rnd [every other rnd] 6 times. (8 sts)

Cut yarn, leaving an 8-inch tail.

Using tapestry needle, thread tail through rem sts and pull tight.

Weave in all ends.

Finishing
Follow basic felting instructions on page 172 until finished measurements are obtained or cozy is desired size. If making cozies in different colors, felt each separately.

Shape by putting over flowerpot and allowing to dry thoroughly; cozy should fit snugly when wet and will conform to the pot's shape as it dries.

When dry, fluff edging. ❄

Festive Felted Christmas Balls

These felted balls can be used in so many decorative ways: as tree ornaments, to dress up a special wreath, or just placed in festive bowls.

■■□□ EASY

Design by Anita Closic

Finished Felted Size

Approx 2-inch diameter
Measurement achieved using yarn and color specified; results may vary depending on yarn, yarn color and felting time.

Materials

- Plymouth Galway Worsted 100 percent wool medium weight yarn (210 yds/100g per ball): 1 ball each fuchsia #141, red #150, marl pink #604, blue #129, purple #153 **4 MEDIUM**
- Size 13 (10mm) straight needles
- Tapestry needle

Pre-Felted Gauge

10 sts and 13 rows = 4 inches/10cm in St st with 2 strands held tog
Exact gauge is not critical; make sure your sts are loose and airy.

Special Abbreviation

Inc (Increase): Inc 1 by knitting in front and back of st.

Pattern Notes

One ball of yarn will make several balls.
Balls are worked with 2 strands of yarn held tog throughout.

Ball

Using 2 strands of yarn held tog, cast on 3 sts leaving an 8-inch tail.
Row 1 (RS): Inc in each st. (6 sts)
Row 2 and all WS rows: Purl.

Row 5: *K1, inc; rep from * across. (18 sts)
Row 7: *K2tog, k1; rep from * across. (12 sts)
Row 9: K2tog across. (6 sts)
Row 11: K2tog across. (3 sts)
Row 12: P3tog. (1 st)
Fasten off and cut yarn leaving a 12-inch tail.

Finishing

Wind tail into a ball and stuff into center.
Sew side seam to form ball, gathering at cast-on end.
Pull tails to inside of ball and cut.
Follow basic felting instructions on page 172 until balls are desired size. ❋

Songbirds

Bring the outdoors inside by hanging songbird ornaments among the boughs of your Christmas tree.

Designs by Celeste Pinheiro

Finished Size
Approx 7 inches long

Materials
- Plymouth Encore Chunky 75 percent acrylic/25 percent wool bulky weight yarn (143 yds/100g per ball): 1 ball each yellow #1382, black #217, white #146, turquoise #235 and red #1386
- Size 9 (5.5mm) straight needles
- 6 (⅜-inch) gold shank buttons (2 for each bird)
- Tapestry needle

Gauge
12 sts and 14 rows = 4 inches/10cm in St st
Exact gauge is not important.

Special Abbreviation
M1 (Make 1): Inc 1 by inserting the LH needle under the horizontal strand between st just worked and next st; knit the strand tbl.

Pattern Notes
Follow instructions for Basic Bird, and *at the same time*, refer to Color Sequences for individual bird color instructions.

If you would like to make smaller birds, use worsted weight yarn and size 7 (4.5mm) needles.

Basic Bird
Tail
Cast on 7 sts.
Row 1 (WS): Purl.

Row 2: *P1, k1; rep from * to last st, end p1.
Rep [Rows 1 and 2] 5 times, work Row 1.

Body
Inc row (RS): K1, M1, knit to last st, M1, k1. (9 sts)
Continue in St st, and rep Inc row [every other row] 4 times. (17 sts)
Work even for 7 rows.
Dec row (RS): K1, k2tog, knit to last 3 sts, ssk, k1. (15 sts)
Continue in St st, and rep Dec row [every other row] twice, ending on a WS row. (11 sts)

Head
Row 1 (RS): K5, M1, k1, M1, k5. (13 sts)
Row 2 and all WS rows: Purl.
Row 3: K6, M1, k1, M1, k6. (15 sts)
Row 5: K1, k2tog, k3, sk2p, k3, ssk, k1. (11 sts)
Row 7: K1, k2tog, k1, sk2p, k1, ssk, k1. (7 sts)

Beak
Change color.
Row 1 and all WS rows: Purl.
Row 2: K1, k2tog, k1, ssk, k1. (5 sts)
Row 4: K1, sk2p, k1. (3 sts)
Cut yarn, leaving a 5-inch tail. Pull through rem sts.

Right Wing
Cast on 5 sts.
Row 1 and all WS rows: Purl.
Row 2 (RS): P1, k1, p1, k1, p1. (5 sts)
Row 4: P1, k1, p1, (k1, p1) in next st, p1. (6 sts)

Row 6: P1, k1, p1, k1, (p1, k1) in next st, p1. (7 sts)
Row 8: P1, k1, p1, k1, p1, k1, p1.
Row 10: P1, k1, p1, k1, ssk, p1. (6 sts)
Row 12: P1, k1, p1, ssk, p1. (5 sts)
Row 14: P1, k1, ssk, p1. (4 sts)
Row 16: P1, ssk, p1. (3 sts)
Row 17: P3tog. (1 st)
Cut yarn, leaving a 4-inch tail.
Fasten off.

Left Wing
Row 1 and all WS rows: Purl.
Row 2 (RS): P1, k1, p1, k1, p1. (5 sts)
Row 4: P1, (p1, k1) in next st, p1, k1, p1. (6 sts)
Row 6: P1, (k1, p1) in next st, k1, p1, k1, p1. (7 sts)
Row 8: P1, k1, p1, k1, p1, k1, p1.
Row 10: P1, k2tog, k1, p1, k1, p1. (6 sts)
Row 12: P1, k2tog, p1, k1, p1. (5 sts)
Row 14: P1, k2tog, k1, p1. (4 sts)
Row 16: P1, k2tog, p1. (3 sts)
Row 17: P3tog. (1 st)
Cut yarn, leaving a 4-inch tail.
Fasten off.

Finishing
Sew belly seam, starting at beak and ending at base of tail; stuff with waste yarn as you sew.
Sew on wings.
Tack tog back of head to base of neck (see Fig. 1).
Sew on buttons for eyes.
Cut 3 strands in red, yellow and white braid and attach to back for hanger.

Color sequences

Cardinal

Tail, Body, Head, Wings: Red.
Beak: Yellow.
Mask: Embroider around eye area using black chain st (see page 65).

Goldfinch

Tail: 8 rows black, 3 rows white.
Body, Head: Yellow.
Beak: White.
Wings: 6 rows yellow, 2 rows black, 2 rows white, work in black to end.
Mask: Embroider around eye area using black chain st.

Blue Jay:

Tail and Body: 2 rows black, *2 rows turquoise, 2 rows black; rep from * twice, continue in turquoise.
Head and Beak: Black.

Wings: *2 rows turquoise, 2 rows black; rep from * twice, work in turquoise to end.
Tuft on crest: Embroider in turquoise. ❆

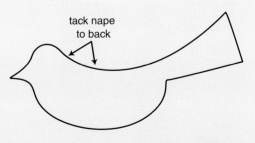

tack nape to back

FIG. 1

Yuletide Jewels

Ribbon yarn and beads transform plain glass ornaments into Yuletide jewels.

Design by Pauline Schultz

Finished Size

Fits around 3½-inch/83mm-diameter ornament

Materials

- Plymouth Jungle 100 percent nylon super bulky weight yarn (61 yds/50g per ball): 1 ball each flame #2, jeweled multi #6 and Plymouth Heavy Metals copper #744
- Size 10.5 (6.5mm) double-pointed needles (set of 4)
- Cable needle
- Tapestry needle
- Crochet hook
- 3 (3½-inch/83mm-diameter) clear glass ball ornaments
- 32 Westrim Crafts style #2856 (5mm) metallic pony beads per ball
- Kreinik Metallics ⅛-inch ribbon to match yarn

Gauge

Gauge is not critical.

Special Abbreviations

C4F (Cross 4 Forward): Dropping extra loops, sl 2 sts to cn and hold in front, k2, k2 from cn.

C4B (Cross 4 Back): Dropping extra loops, sl 2 sts to cn and hold in back, k2, k2 from cn.

CDD (Centered double dec): Sl next 2 sts tog knitwise, k1, pass 2 slipped sts over.

Special Technique

I-cord: *K3, do not turn, sl sts back to LH needle; rep from * until cord is desired length. Bind off.

Ornament Cover

Cast on 6 sts.

Distribute on 3 dpns and join without twisting; place marker between first and last sts.

Rnd 1: Yo, k1 around. (12 sts)

Rnd 2: Knit.

Rnds 3–6: Rep Rnds 1 and 2. (48 sts)

Rnds 7, 9 and 11: Knit, winding yarn twice around RH needle.

Rnd 8: C4F around.

Rnd 10: C4B around.

Rnd 12: C4F around.

Rnd 13: [Yo, CDD] around. (32 sts)

Rnd 14: Knit.

Rnd 15: K2tog around. (16 sts)

Rnd 16: Knit.

Measure off approx 80 inches of yarn.

Using tapestry needle, thread yarn through sts; do not tighten.

Remove needles.

Discard metal top and insert ornament, bottom first.

Pull sts tight over neck of ornament and secure.

Without cutting yarn, pick up and knit 3 sts at top.

Work I-cord until approx 6 inches of yarn rem. Bind off.

Sew top of I-cord to top of ornament, making loop; secure and cut yarn.

Finishing

Tighten cast-on sts.

Cut 4 (12-inch) strands of yarn.

Using a crochet hook, fold each strand in half and attach to the bottom of the ornament as you would for fringe.

Trim ends on the diagonal.

String 16 beads on ⅛-inch ribbon in colors as desired. Tie between base of ball and fringe; secure. Rep at I-cord joining. ❄

Wreath Table Trimmings

Adorn your holiday table with these colorful felted wreaths surrounding napkins and votive candles.

Designs by Posey Salem

■■□□ EASY

Finished Felted Sizes

Votive Ring: 3-inch outer diameter; 2-inch center hole diameter

Napkin Ring: 2½-inch outer diameter; 1½-inch center hole diameter

Materials

- Plymouth Galway Worsted 100 percent wool medium weight yarn (210 yds/100g per ball): 1 ball each off-white #1 (A), green #17 (B), and red #16 (C) for 4–6 rings
- Size 8 (5mm) straight needles
- Size 15 (10mm) straight needles
- Tapestry needle
- Glass votive holder for blocking (optional)
- Empty bathroom tissue cardboard core for blocking (optional)

Gauge

Exact gauge is not critical; make sure your sts are loose and airy.

Special Abbreviation

Inc (Increase): Inc 1 by knitting into the front and back of st.

Pattern Note

Make 1 wreath, 2 leaves and 1 berry per ring.

Finished Felted Sizes are achieved using yarn and colors specified; results may vary depending on yarn, yarn color and felting time.

Napkin-Ring Wreath

With larger needles and 3 strands A, B or C held tog, cast on 4 sts.

I-cord: *K4, do not turn, sl sts back to LH needle; rep from * until cord is 7½ inches.

Bind off.

Sew ends of I-cord tog to form ring. Weave in yarn tails.

Votive Ring Wreath

Work as for Napkin Ring Wreath, but make I-cord 8 inches.

Leaves

With smaller needles and 1 strand of A or B, cast on 2 sts.

Row 1 (RS): Inc in each st. (4 sts)

Row 2 and all WS rows: Purl.

Row 3: Inc, k2, inc. (6 sts)

Rows 5 and 7: Knit.

Row 9: Ssk, k2, k2tog. (4 sts)

Row 11: Ssk, k2tog. (2 sts)

Row 12: P2tog. (1 st)

Fasten off and weave in tails.

Berry

With smaller needles and 1 strand of A or C, cast on 1 st.

Row 1 (WS): (Inc in each st) 3 times. (6 sts)

Rows 2 and 4: Purl.

Rows 3 and 5: Knit.

Row 6: [P2tog] 3 times. (3 sts)

Row 7: Sl 1, k2tog, psso. (1 st)

Fasten off, leaving an 8-inch tail.

With RS (purl side) facing, use tail to sew sides and gather as necessary to form a ball.

Finishing

Arrange leaves and berries over the sewn ends of wreath and sew securely to front side of ring with matching yarn.

Weave in all ends.

Follow basic felting instructions on page 172 until finished measurements are obtained or rings are desired size.

Shape rings, allowing Votive Rings to dry over glass votive holder and Napkin Rings around an empty toilet tissue cardboard core. ❋

Great Bags for Giving

These clever bags will be used year after year for superb gift presentations.

 EASY

Designs by Celeste Pinheiro

Finished Sizes
Large Bag: 10 inches wide x 13 inches long

Small Bag (Snowman): 6½ inches wide x 9 inches long

Wine Bottle Bag: 10 inch circumference x 10 inches long

Materials
- Plymouth Encore Worsted 75 percent acrylic/25 percent wool medium weight yarn (200 yds/100g per ball): 1 ball each moss #4379 (A), blue-green #670 (B), red #1386 (C), magenta #1385 (D) and natural #146 (E)
- Size 6 (4mm) straight needles
- Size 8 (5mm) straight needles or size needed to obtain gauge
- Size H/8 (5mm) crochet hook
- Tapestry needle
- Buttons: 6 (½-inch) pearl, 1 (1-inch) pearl, 5 (⅜-inch) black and 16 (⅜–½-inch) pink and red
- Tapestry needle

Gauge
20 sts and 24 rows = 4 inches/10cm in St st with larger needles
To save time, take time to check gauge.

Special Technique
I-Cord: Cast on 3 sts, *k3, do not turn, sl sts back to LH needle; rep from * until cord is desired length. Bind off.

Pattern Note
Use crochet hook and chain st to "draw" embellishments on bags, following figures.

Large Bag
Front
With smaller needles and C, cast on 50 sts. Knit 17 rows.

Change to larger needles and A.

Work 2 rows St st, beg with a RS row.

Eyelet row (RS): K1, *k2tog, yo; rep from * to last st, k1.

Continue in St st until bag measures 13 inches from beg, ending with a WS row.

Bottom Shaping
Row 1 (RS): K5, sk2p, knit to last 8 sts, sk2p, k5. (46 sts)

Row 2 and all WS rows: Purl.

Row 3: K4, sk2p, knit to last 7 sts, sk2p, k4. (42 sts)

Row 5: K3, sk2p, knit to last 6 sts, sk2p, k3. (38 sts)

Row 7: K2, sk2p, knit to last 5 sts, sk2p, k2. (34 sts)

Row 9: K1, sk2p, knit to last 4 sts, sk2p, k1. (30 sts)

Bind off.

Back
Work as for front.

Finishing
Weave in all ends.

Referring to Fig. 1, use crochet hook and chain st to "draw" tree with B and "MeRRY" with D. Use tapestry needle and E to embroider snowflakes. Sew on 16 pink and red buttons with E.

Sew side and bottom seams.

With D, work I-cord for 30 inches.

Thread through eyelets, tie overhand knot in ends, tie in bow.

Small Bag
Stripe Pattern
Row 1 (RS): With C, purl.

Rows 2–6: With C, work in St st.

Row 7: With D, purl.

Rows 8-12: With D, work in St st.

Rep Rows 1–12 for pat.

Front
With smaller needles and B, cast on 34 sts.

Knit 17 rows.

Change to larger needles and D.

Work 2 rows in St st, beg with a RS row.

Eyelet row (RS): K1, *k2tog, yo; rep from * to last st, k1.

Work 7 rows in St st.

Change to C and work Stripe Pat until piece measures approx 9 inches from beg, ending with Row 6 or 12.

Bottom shaping
Continue with last color used and work bottom as for large bag, beg with Row 3, ending with 22 sts.

Bind off.

Back
Work as for front.

Finishing
Weave in all ends.

Referring to Fig. 2 for placement, use crochet hook and chain st to "draw" snowman outline with E, arms and mouth with B; sew on black buttons for eyes with D, and for front buttons with A.

Sew side and bottom seams.

With A, work I-cord for 25 inches.

Thread through eyelets, tie overhand knot in ends, tie in bow.

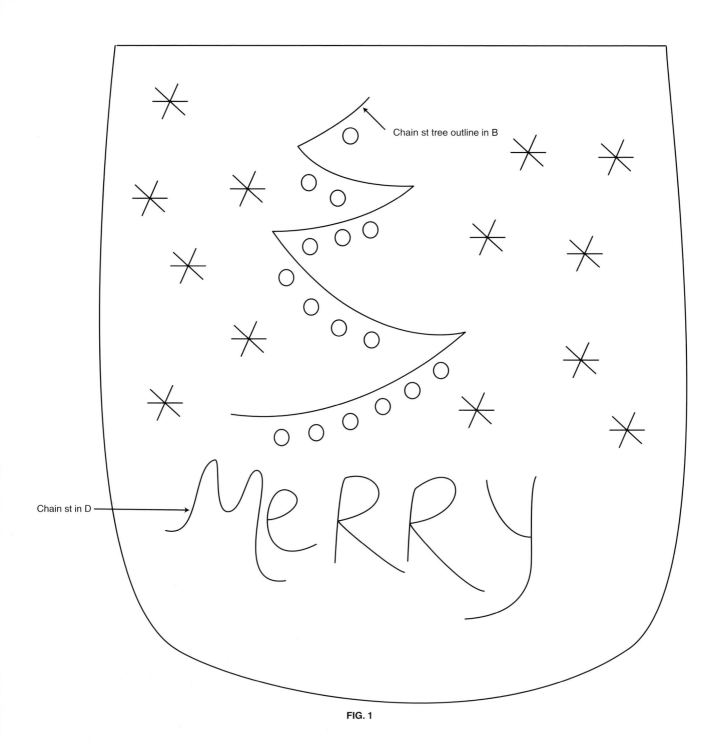

Chain st tree outline in B

Chain st in D

FIG. 1

Wine Bag

With smaller needles and A, cast on 50 sts.

Knit 17 rows.

Change to larger needles and B.

Work 2 rows in St st, beg with a RS row.

Eyelet row (RS): K1, *k2tog, yo; rep from * to last st, k1.

Work 3 rows in St st.

Next row (RS): Beg working Fair Isle chart and continue until bag measures 10 inches from beg, ending with a WS row.

Bottom Shaping

Cut D and continue with B only.

Row 1 (RS): * K5, k2tog, place marker; rep from * to last st, k1. (43 sts).

Row 2 and all WS rows: Purl.

Dec row: *Knit to 2 sts before marker, k2tog; rep from * to last st, k1. (36 sts) Rep Dec row every RS row until 8 sts rem.

Cut yarn, leaving a 5-inch tail.

Using tapestry needle, thread tail through rem sts, and pull tight.

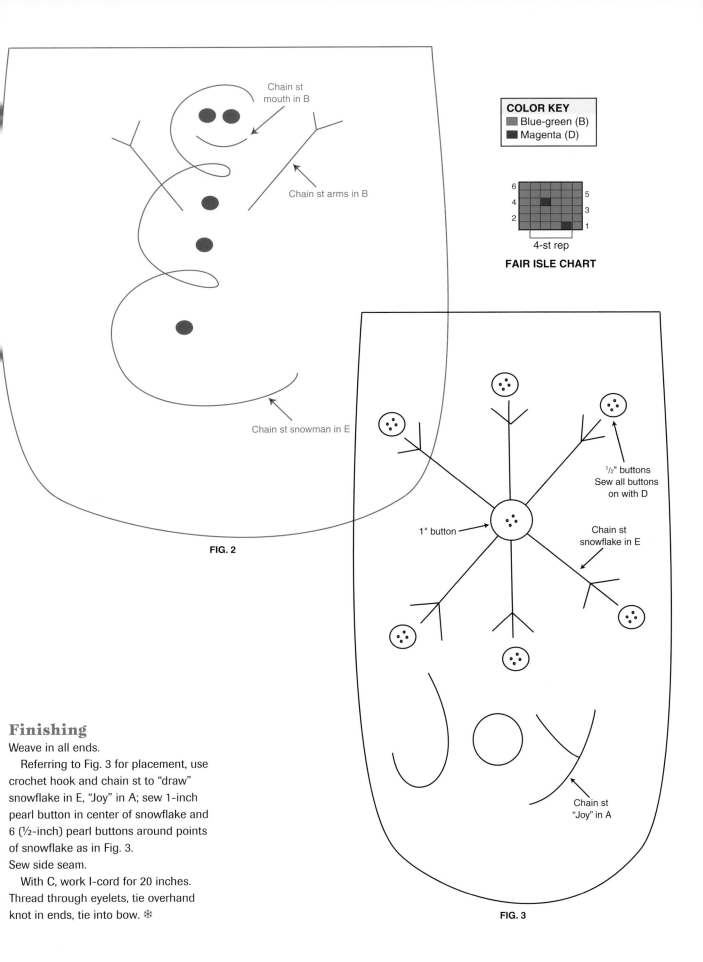

Chain st
mouth in B

Chain st arms in B

Chain st snowman in E

FIG. 2

COLOR KEY
▨ Blue-green (B)
■ Magenta (D)

FAIR ISLE CHART

4-st rep

½" buttons
Sew all buttons
on with D

1" button

Chain st
snowflake in E

Chain st
"Joy" in A

FIG. 3

Finishing

Weave in all ends.

Referring to Fig. 3 for placement, use crochet hook and chain st to "draw" snowflake in E, "Joy" in A; sew 1-inch pearl button in center of snowflake and 6 (½-inch) pearl buttons around points of snowflake as in Fig. 3.
Sew side seam.

With C, work I-cord for 20 inches. Thread through eyelets, tie overhand knot in ends, tie into bow. ❄

Flurry of Fun Pillows

Enjoy the warmth inside while looking at snowy Christmas-tree and snowman scenes on your pillows.

◼◼◼◻ INTERMEDIATE

Designs by Sara Louise Harper

Finished Size
Fits 14 x 10 inch pillow form

Materials
Christmas Tree Pillow
- Plymouth Galway Worsted 100 percent wool medium weight yarn (210 yds/100g per ball): 2 balls dark red #148 (A)
- Plymouth Tweed 100 percent virgin lamb's wool medium weight yarn (109 yds/50g per ball): 1 ball each cream #5302 (B), brown #5277 (C) and green #5314 (D)

- Size 7 (4.5mm) straight needles or size needed to obtain gauge
- Size 8 (5mm) straight needles or size needed to obtain gauge

Snowman Pillow
- Plymouth Tweed 100 percent virgin lamb's wool medium weight yarn (109 yds/50g per ball): 3 balls gray #5309 (A), 2 balls cream #5302 (B) and small amount green #5314 (D)
- Plymouth Galway Worsted 100 percent wool medium weight yarn (210 yds/100g per ball): 1 ball dark red #148 (C)

- Size 8 (5mm) straight needles or size needed to obtain gauge

Both Pillows
- Size G/7 (4.5mm) crochet hook
- 6 (1-inch) star buttons
- Tapestry needle
- 2 (12 x 16-inch) pillow forms*

*Sample uses Soft Touch by Fairfield

Gauge
19 sts and 21 rows = 4 inches/10cm in St st with larger needles and Galway Worsted

17 sts and 19 rows = 4 inches/10cm in St st with larger needles and Plymouth Tweed

To save time, take time to check gauge.

Pattern Notes
Pillow is worked in 1 piece, and then folded and closed in the back with buttons (see Fig. 1).

Work selvage sts (first and last sts) in garter st; in colorwork area, knit the edge sts using both yarns.

Snowman's scarf is knit separately, then attached; his eyes are cross-stitches

Christmas Trees Pillow
With larger needles and A, cast on 78 sts.

Row 1 (RS): *K1, p1; rep from * across.

Row 2: Purl.

Work in St st until piece measures 6 inches from beg, ending with a WS row.

Change to smaller needles, and work Chart A.

With larger needles and A, work in St st for 7 inches, ending with a WS row.

Last row: *K1, p1; rep from * across. Bind off all sts.

Finishing

Weave in all ends.

Button Closures

With A, crochet 3 chains approx 2½ inches long.

Attach 2 chains to top of pillow 1 inch from each end and attach 3rd chain in the middle, adjusting the length of chains to fit snugly around your buttons.

Lay flat and block, allowing to dry thoroughly.

Place pillow cover on pillow form and pin closed, marking spots for buttons opposite chains.

Remove carefully from form and seam.

Attach buttons and re-insert pillow form.

Snowman Pillow

With larger needles and A, cast on 66 sts.

Work as for Christmas Tree Pillow, but use larger needles throughout and work Chart B instead of Chart A.

Embellishments

With D, work cross-stitches for snowman's eyes where indicated on Chart B.

Scarf: With C, cast on 3 sts and work in St st to desired length.

Sew to pillow as in picture, then work

2 parallel long sts at neck edge to form "scarf knot."

Finish as for Christmas Tree Pillow, making button closure chains with A. ❆

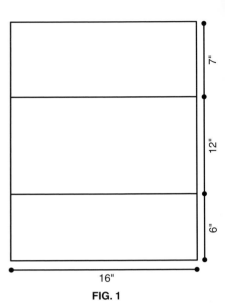

FIG. 1

COLOR KEY
- ■ Red (A)
- □ Cream (B)
- ▨ Brown (C)
- ■ Green (D)

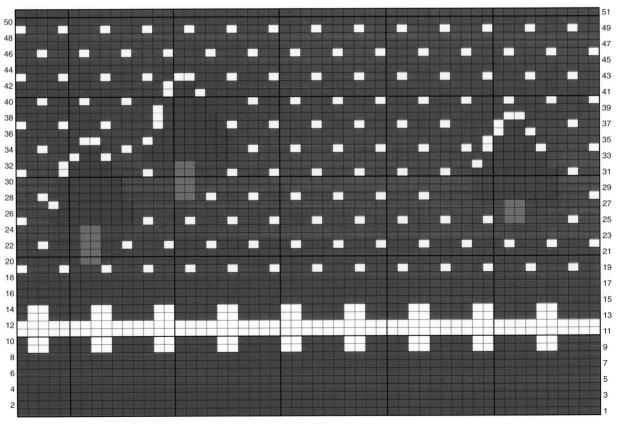

CHART A

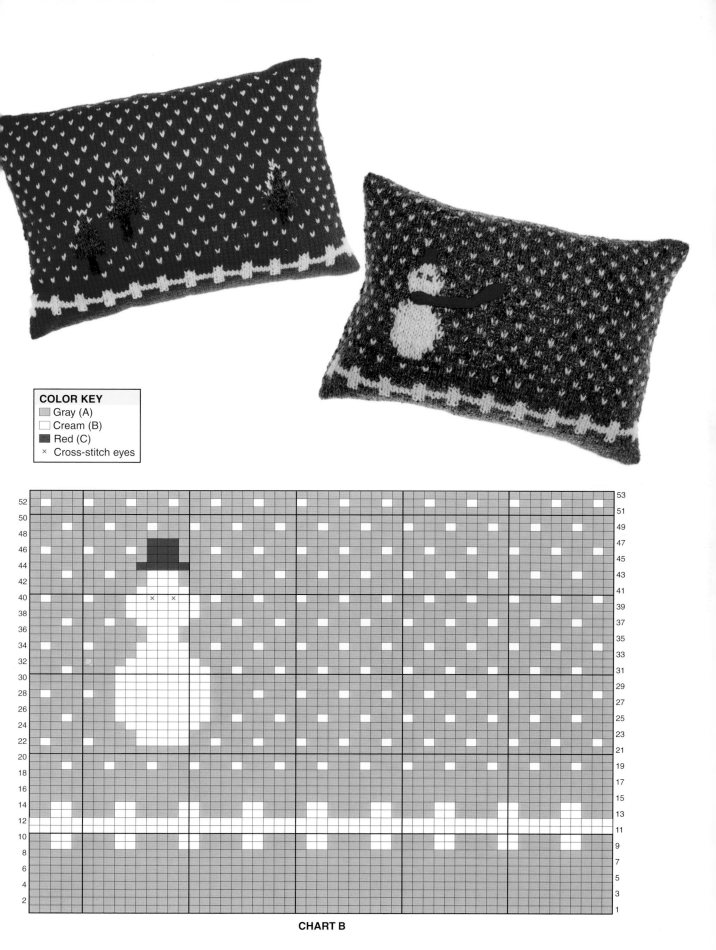

COLOR KEY
- ▨ Gray (A)
- ☐ Cream (B)
- ■ Red (C)
- × Cross-stitch eyes

CHART B

Lacework Mantel Scarf

Set an elegant tone with this beautiful mantel scarf featuring a clever Christmas tree edging.

▰▰▰▱ INTERMEDIATE

Design by Sara Louise Harper

Finished Size

12 x 54 (12 x 60, 12 x 66) inches
Instructions are given for smallest size, with larger sizes in parenthesis. When only 1 number is given, it applies to all sizes.

Materials

- Plymouth Merino Supreme 100 percent merino wool medium weight yarn (64 yds/50g per ball): 7 (8, 9) balls green #2222
- Size 9 (5.5mm) 29-inch circular needle or size needed to obtain gauge
- Tapestry needle

Gauge

16 sts and 22 rows = 4 inches/10cm in St st
To save time, take time to check gauge.

Pattern Notes

This mantel scarf is worked side to side; a circular needle is used to accommodate the large number of sts—do not join.

Each 10-st lace rep measures approx 2½ inches; if you need to adjust length of scarf to fit your mantel, cast on 10 more or fewer sts for every 2½ inches of desired adjustment.

Special Abbreviation

MB (Make Bobble): [P1, k1, p1] in next st, turn; k1, p1, k1, turn; k1, p1, k1, pass first and 2nd sts over 3rd st.

Mantel Scarf

Cast on 191 (221, 261) sts.
Row 1 (WS): *P5, MB, p4; rep from * to last st, p1.
Row 2: K1, *yo, k3, sk2p, k3, yo, k1; rep from * across.

Row 3: Purl.
Row 4: P1, *k1, yo, k2, sk2p, k2, yo, k1, p1; rep from * across.
Rows 5, 7, 9: K1, *p9, k1; rep from * across.
Row 6: P1, *k2, yo, k1, sk2p, k1, yo, k2, p1; rep from * across.
Row 8: P1, *k3, yo, sk2p, yo, k3, p1; rep from * across.
Row 10: Knit.
Row 11: K1, purl to last st, k1.

Continue in St st, maintaining first and last st in garter st for edge, until piece measures 12 inches or desired depth for mantel.

Bind off.

Weave in ends.

Block gently by pinning each bobble and stretching slightly to elongate the lace section; mist thoroughly and allow to dry. ❄

Peppermint Posers

These little faux candies look good enough to eat!

◼◼◻◻◻ EASY

Design by Ellen Edwards Drechsler

Finished Size

4 inches long (including tied ends)

Materials

- Plymouth Encore D.K. 75 percent acrylic/25 percent wool light weight yarn (150 yds/50g per ball): 1 ball each red #1386 (MC) or green #54 (MC) and white #146 (CC)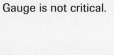
- Size 4 (3.5mm) straight needles or size needed to obtain gauge
- Fiberfill or yarn scraps
- ¼-inch-wide white ribbon
- Tapestry needle

Gauge

21 sts and 26 rows = 4 inches/10cm in St st
Gauge is not critical.

Special Abbreviation

Inc (Increase): Inc 1 by working p1, k1 in same st.

Pattern Stitch

Stripes

*In St st, work 2 rows MC, 2 rows CC; rep from * for Stripes Pat.

Pattern Notes

Use either red or green as MC, as desired.

Work Stripes Pat throughout.

When working stripes, do not cut yarn; carry yarn not in use up side.

Candies

With MC, cast on 3 sts.

Work 3 rows Stripes Pat.

Inc row (WS): Inc, purl to last st, inc. (5 sts)

Rep Inc row [every WS row] 6 times. (17 sts)

Work even until you've finished 7 stripes of each color.

Dec row (WS): Ssp, purl to last 2 sts, p2tog. (15 sts)

Rep Dec row [every WS row] 6 times. (3 sts)

Work 2 rows even.

Next row (RS): Sl 1, k2tog, psso. (1 st)

Cut yarn and fasten off.

Finishing

Sew long sides tog to form a tube.

Weave in ends.

Stuff the middle with fiberfill or yarn scraps.

Tie ribbons at each end as shown. ❄

Peppermint & Holly Doorstop

This striped doorstop cover mimics a piece of wrapped peppermint candy.

 EASY

Design by Posey Salem

Finished Size
14½ x 3½ x 2½ inches (stuffed)

Materials
- Plymouth Galway Worsted 100 percent wool medium weight yarn (210 yds/100g per ball): 1 ball each off-white #01 (A), red #16 (B) and green #17 (C)
- Size 6 (4mm) straight needles
- Size 8 (5mm) straight needles or size needed to obtain gauge
- 2 stitch markers
- Tapestry needle
- 1 sheet of white plastic canvas
- Clean pebbles (to use as weight, optional)
- Crumpled white tissue paper (to use as filler, optional)

Gauge
18 sts and 24 rows = 4 inches/10cm in St st with larger needles
To save time, take time to check gauge.

Special Abbreviations
M1 (Make 1): Inc by making a backward loop over RH needle.
Inc (Increase): Inc 1 by knitting in front and back of st.

Pattern Stitches
A. Seed St (even number of sts)
Row 1 (WS): *P1, k1; rep from * to end.
Row 2: *K1, p1; rep from * to end.
    Rep Rows 1 and 2 for pat.
B. Stripe Pat
    Working in St st, *work 2 rows B, then 2 rows A; rep from * for stripes.

Pattern Note
Holly embellishment is knit separately, then sewn in place.

Wrapper
First Ruffle
With larger needles and A, cast on 76 sts.
    Work 4 rows in Seed St.
Next row (WS): Purl.
    Work 4 rows even in Stripe Pat.
    Continue in Stripe Pat and dec as follows:
Dec row (RS): K2, [ssk, k21] twice, k2tog, k22, k2tog, k2. (72 sts)
    Work 3 rows even.
Dec row: K7, [ssk, k6] 4 times, [k2tog, k6] 4 times, k1. (64 sts)
    Work 3 rows even.

Dec row: K3, [ssk, k3] 6 times, [k2tog, k3] 5 times, k2tog, k4. (52 sts)
Purl 1 row.

Ribbing
With smaller needles and A only, work 4 rows in k1, p1 rib.

Main Section
With larger needles, work even in Stripe Pat for 58 rows. (14 stripes B, 13 stripes A)

Ribbing
With smaller needles and A only, work 4 rows in k1, p1 rib.

Second Ruffle
With larger needles, continue in Stripe Pat and inc as follows:
Inc row (RS): K4, [M1, k4] 12 times. (64 sts)
Work 3 rows even.
Inc row: K4, [M1, k8] 7 times, M1, k4. (72 sts)
Work 3 rows even.
Row 9: K9, [M1, k18] 3 times, M1, k9. (76 sts)
Work 6 rows even.
With A only, work 4 rows in Seed St. Bind off loosely.
Sew sides tog to form a tube.
Weave in ends.

Embellishments
I-Cord Ties
Make 2
With larger needles and C, cast on 3 sts.
*K3, do not turn, sl sts back to LH needle; rep from * until I-cord measures 15 inches. Bind off.

Holly Leaves
Make 2
With larger needles and C, cast on 3 sts.
Row 1 (RS): K1, [inc, k1] twice. (5 sts)
Rows 2, 4, 6, 8: Purl.
Row 3: K2, yo, k1, yo, k2. (7 sts)
Row 5: K3, yo, k1, yo, k3. (9 sts)
Row 7: K4, yo, k1, yo, k4. (11 sts)
Row 9: Bind off 3 (1 st on RH needle), [k1, yo] twice, k5. (10 sts)
Row 10: Bind off 3, purl to end. (7 sts)
Row 11: K3, yo, k1, yo, k3. (9 sts)
Rows 12 and 14: Purl.
Row 13: K4, yo, k1, yo, k4. (11 sts)
Row 15: Bind off 3, knit to end. (8 sts)
Row 16: Bind off 3, purl to end. (5 sts)
Row 17: Ssk, k1, k2tog. (3 sts)
Row 18: Sl 1, p2tog, psso. (1 st)
Cut yarn and fasten off.
Weave in ends.

Holly Berries
Make 3
With larger needles and B and leaving a 12-inch tail, cast on 3 sts.
Row 1 (WS): Inc, k1, inc. (5 sts)
Rows 2, 4, 6: Purl.
Row 3: Inc, k3, inc. (7 sts)
Rows 5 and 7: Knit.
Row 8: [P2tog] 3 times, p1. (4 sts)
Row 9: [K2tog] twice. (2 sts)
Bind off 2 sts.
Turn berries purl-side out.
With tapestry needle and cast-on tail, sew and gather sides tog into a ball shape.
Weave in ends.

Finishing
Plastic Box
Cut plastic canvas as follows:
2 pieces: 2⁵⁄₁₆ X 3³⁄₁₆ inches
2 pieces: 2⁵⁄₁₆ X 7 inches
2 pieces: 3³⁄₁₆ X 7 inches
With tapestry needle and A, sew plastic canvas pieces tog to form a rectangular box, leaving 1 end open and hinged on 1 side only.
To weight the box, fill with pebbles or stuff with crumpled tissue paper. Close end flap and sew shut.

Assembly
Insert plastic canvas box into tube and center between ribbed sections.
Arrange holly leaves and berries on center top (see photo), and pin in place.
Remove box and using matching yarn, tack the leaves and berries in place.
Reinsert box, centered as before. Tie I-cords in bow around ribbed sections to close. ❋

Knitter's Christmas

What knitter could resist "dressing" her tree with these mini-garments and cabled garland? Give these to your knitting friends!

◼◼◼◻ INTERMEDIATE

Designs by Sara Louise Harper

Finished Sizes
Sock: 2 x 4 inches
Mitten: 2½ x 4 inches
Sweater: 2½ x 3 inches
Garland: Approx 1 inch wide, length as desired

Materials
- Plymouth Country 8 Ply 100 percent superwash wool medium weight yarn (105 yards/50g per ball): 1 ball each red #1872 (A), purple #2246 (B), green #2250 (C), pink #1977 (D), yellow #1085 (E) and lilac #2246 (F) (makes 8 feet of garland)
- Size 6 (4mm) straight and double-pointed needles or size needed to obtain gauge
- Stitch markers, 1 in CC for beg of rnd
- Tapestry needle

Gauge
20 sts and 28 rows = 4 inches/10cm in St st
To save time, take time to check gauge.

Special Abbreviations
N1, N2, N3: Needle 1, Needle 2, Needle 3
M1 (Make 1): Insert LH needle from front to back under the horizontal strand between the last st worked and next st on LH needle. With RH needle, knit into the back of this loop.

Stitch Patterns
A. K1, P1, Rib (in-the-round on even number of stitches)
Row 1: *K1, p1; rep from * around.
   Rep Row 1 for pat.
B. K1, P1 Rib (in rows on odd number of sts)
Row 1: K1, *p1, k1; rep from * across.

Row 2: P1, *k1, p1, rep from * across.
   Rep Rows 1 and 2 for pat.
C. Seed St (in rows on odd number of sts)
Row 1: K1, *p1, k1; rep from * to end.
   Rep Row 1 for pat.
D. Seed St (in-the-round on even number of sts)
Rnd 1: *K1, p1; rep from * around.
Rnd 2: *P1, k1; rep from * around.
   Rep Rnds 1 and 2 for pat.

Pattern Notes
One ball of each color will make 5 or 6 ornaments.

Each pat is written as a "Basic" single-colored version, followed by multi-colored versions.

Basic Mitten
Cuff

With A, cast on 24 sts. Distribute sts evenly on 3 dpns and join without twisting; place marker between first and last sts.

Work 5 rnds in K1, P1 Rib.
Work 6 rnds in St st.

Thumb Gusset

K11, place marker, k2, place marker, knit 11.

Rnd 1: Knit to marker, sl marker, M1, knit to next marker, M1, knit to end of rnd. (26 sts)
Rnd 2: Knit.

Rep Rnds 1 and 2 until there are 8 sts between markers for gusset; place these sts on waste yarn for holder.

Hand

Work even in St st on rem 22 sts until mitten measures 4 inches from beg.
Next rnd: *K2, k2tog; rep from * to last 2 sts, k2. (17 sts)

Knit 1 rnd.
Next rnd: *K2tog, k1; rep from * to last 2 sts, k2tog. (11 sts)

Knit 1 rnd.
Next rnd: K2tog around, end k1. (6 sts)

Cut yarn, leaving a 10-inch tail.
Using tapestry needle, thread tail through rem sts, and pull tight. Weave in all ends on WS.

Thumb

Distribute 8 sts on holder on 3 dpns; join and place marker between first and last sts.

Attach yarn, and work 4 rnds in St st.
Next rnd: K2tog around. (4 sts)

Using tapestry needle, thread tail through rem sts, and pull tight.
Weave in all ends on WS.
Braid 3 lengths of yarn and pull through top of mitten to hang.

Striped Mitten

Work as for Basic Mitten in following stripe sequence:
2 rnds each A, B, D, C, E.

Duplicate-Stitch Mitten
Cuff

With D, cast on 24 sts. Distribute sts evenly on 3 dpns and join without twisting; place marker between first and last sts.

Purl 1 rnd D; purl 1 rnd C; knit 1 rnd A; purl 1 rnd D; purl 1 rnd C.
With A, work 6 rnds in St st.

Thumb Gusset

K11 A, place marker, k2 C, place marker, k11 A. Continue to work gusset as for Basic Mitten, loosely draping C across gusset area to bring it into proper position on each succeeding rnd.

Complete Hand as for Basic Mitten.
Work Thumb in C as for Basic Mitten.

Duplicate-Stitch Accents

With D, work duplicate sts (see illustration on page 109) randomly over red area.

Braid 3 lengths of yarn and pull through top of mitten to hang.

Basic Sock
Leg

With A, cast on 18 sts. Distribute sts evenly on 3 dpns and join without twisting; place marker between first and last sts.

Work 5 rnds in K1, P1 Rib.
Work 10 rnds in St st.

Heel

Sl 8 sts to first dpn, 5 sts to 2nd dpn and 5 sts to 3rd dpn.

Work back and forth in rows on first dpn as follows:

Row 1 (RS): *Sl 1, k1; rep from * across.

Row 2: Sl 1, purl across.

[Rep Rows 1 and 2] 3 times, work Row 1.

Heel Turn

Row 1 (WS): P5, p2tog, p1, turn.

Row 2: Sl 1, k1, ssk, k2, turn.

Row 3: Sl 1, p1, p2tog, p1, turn.

Row 4: Sl 1, k1, ssk, k1. (4 sts)

Gusset

With RS facing and using same needle (now N1), pick up and knit 5 sts along side of heel; with N2, k10 from next 2 dpns; with N3, pick up and knit 5 sts along other side of heel, k2 from N1. (24 sts)

Rnd 1: N1: knit to last 2 sts, k2tog; N2: knit; N3: ssk, knit to end. (22 sts)

Rnd 2: Knit.

Rep Rnds 1 and 2 until 16 sts rem.

Foot

Work even in St st for 6 rnds.

Toe

Sl 1 st from beg of N2 to N1; sl 1 st from end of N2 to N3. (16 sts arranged N1: 4 sts, N2: 8 sts, N3: 4 sts)

Rnd 1: N1: knit to last 2 sts, k2tog; N2: ssk, knit to last 2 sts, k2tog; N3: ssk, knit to end. (12 sts)

Rnd 2: Knit.

Rep Rnds 1 and 2. (8 sts)

With N3, k2 from N1.

Cut yarn, leaving an 8-inch tail.

Finishing

Graft toe tog with Kitchener st. (see page 173)

Weave in all ends.

Stuff sock with fiberfill or a small plastic cylinder (like a pill container) if desired.

Braid 3 lengths of yarn, and pull through top back of sock to hang.

Color-Block Sock

Work as for Basic Sock, changing colors as follows:

Work Rib with C, then work rem rnds of Leg with A.

Work Heel, Gusset and first 4 rnds of Foot with E.

Work last 2 rnds of Foot and Toe with C.

Basic Sweater
Body

With straight needles and A, cast on 15 sts.

Work 4 rows in K1, P1 Rib.

Work 8 rows in St st.

Begin Sleeves

Work in St st across next 2 rows, and cast on 7 sts at end of each row. (29 sts)

Work 4 rows in St st.

Neck Opening
Next row (RS): K12, bind off 5 sts, k12.
Next row: P12, cast on 5 sts over the bound-off sts, p12.
Work 4 rows in St st.

End Sleeves
Bind off 7 sts at beg of next 2 rows. (15 sts)
Work 8 rows in St st.
Work 4 rows in K1, P1 Rib.
Bind off in rib.
Cut yarn, leaving a long tail for seaming.

Cuffs
Pick up and knit 9 sts along edge of each sleeve.
Work 2 rows in K1, P1 Rib.
Bind off in rib.

Turtleneck
With dpns, pick up and knit 12 sts around neck; join.
Work 3 rnds in K1, P1 Rib.
Bind off in rib.

Finishing
Sew side and sleeve seams.
Weave in all ends on WS.

Sweater with Two-Color Rib
Work as for Basic Sweater using colors as indicated.
With straight needles and C, cast on 15 sts.
Work 4 rows in K1 A, P1 C Rib.
Complete Body and Sleeves with E, ending before final rib.
Work 4 rows in K1 A, P1 C Rib.
With C, bind off in rib.
Work Cuffs and Turtleneck in K1 A, P1 C Rib, binding off each with C.

Stranded-Color Sweater
Work as for Basic Sweater using colors and pats indicated.
With straight needles and E, cast on 15 sts.

Work in Seed St for 4 rows.
Work chart in C and D over next 6 rows.
With B, work 2 rows St st.
Continue as for Basic Sweater until 2 rows past end of Sleeves.
Work chart in C and D over next 6 rows.
With B, work in Seed St for 4 rows.
Bind off in Seed St.

Cuffs
With E, pick up and knit 9 sts along edge of each sleeve.
Work 2 rows in Seed St.
Bind off in Seed St.

Turtleneck
With dpns and E, pick up and knit 12 sts around neck; join.
Work 3 rnds in Seed St.
Bind off in Seed St.
Finish as for Basic Sweater.

Cable Garland
Special Technique
Tack 1 st: With LH needle, reach under and pick up loop (or running thread) formed by making cable turn, then knit it tog with 2nd st on cn.

Pattern Notes
Gauge is not critical, but be sure to keep gauge consistent.
Garland will not lay flat if a tacking st is not taken during cable turn. Therefore, when turning cable, take a "tacking st" by working a k2tog with 2nd st on cable needle and the horizontal running thread between the 2 sets of 3 sts made when turning cable.

Garland
With F, cast on 6 sts.
Rows 1, 3 and 7 (RS): K6.
Rows 2, 4, 6 and 8: P6.
Row 5: Sl 3 sts to cn hand hold in back, k3, k1 from cn, tack 1 st, k1 from cn.
Rep Rows 1–8 until garland reaches desired length.

Bind off all sts.
Weave in all ends.
Steam-block flat and allow to dry. ❄

STRANDED-COLOR SWEATER

COLOR KEY
■ Green (C)
■ Pink (D)

DUPLICATE STITCH
From underneath piece, bring yarn up in the center of the stitch below the stitch to be duplicated. Place needle from right to left behind both sides of the stitch above the one being duplicated, and pull yarn through (a). Complete the stitch by returning the needle to where you began (b).

Razzle-Dazzle Tree Skirt

Break free of tradition! Wrap the bottom of your tree in purple, magenta and gold instead of green and red.

◼◼◻◻ EASY

Design by Scarlet Taylor

Finished Size

Approx 46-inch diameter

Materials

- Plymouth Galway Worsted 100 percent wool medium weight yarn (210 yds/100g per ball): 2 balls magenta #141 (A)
- Plymouth Galway Chunky 100 percent wool bulky weight yarn (123 yds/100g per ball): 7 balls magenta #141 (B)
- Plymouth Stars 50 percent rayon/50 percent nylon medium weight yarn (71 yds/50g per ball): 5 balls purple #106 (C)
- Size 8 (5mm) straight needles
- Size 10 (6mm) straight needles or size needed to obtain gauge
- 6 stitch holders
- Tapestry needle
- Fabric glue
- Materials for felted stars (see page 58)

Gauge

15 sts and 21 rows = 4 inches/10cm in St st with larger needles and B
To save time, take time to check gauge.

Pattern Notes

Tree skirt is made in 6 panels (wedges). The panels are then sewn tog, leaving 1 slit open, allowing skirt to wrap around tree.

Instructions for felted stars are on page 58.

Tree Skirt

Panel

Make 6
With smaller needles and 1 strand each of A and C held tog, cast on 83 sts.

Work 3 rows in garter st.

Dec row (RS): K1, ssk, knit to last 3 sts, k2tog, k1. (81 sts)

Continue in garter st, and rep Dec row [every 4th row] 3 times. (75 sts)

Knit 1 WS row.

Cut A and C.

Change to larger needles and B.
Beg working in St st, and continue to work Dec row [every 4th row] 10 times more, then [every other row] 22 times. (11 sts)

Place sts on holder.

Finishing

Sew panels tog, leaving last 2 edges un-sewn for back slit opening.

Outside edge: With smaller needles and 1 strand each of A and C held tog, knit across all sts from holders. (66 sts)

Knit 3 rows.

Bind off knitwise.

Back opening edges: With smaller needles and B, pick up and knit 76 sts along edge of back opening.

Knit 3 rows.

Bind off knitwise.

Rep for opposite edge.

Weave in yarn ends.

Make felted stars (see page 58) and glue on randomly as desired. ❋

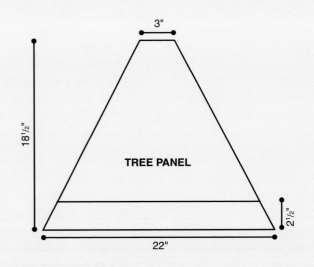

TREE PANEL

3"

18½"

22"

2½"

For coordinating Razzle-Dazzle 'Em
Stocking pattern, see page 57.

Christmas Rose

Red roses in winter? These easy-knit and felted flowers are a fun alternative to the poinsettia.

■■■▢ INTERMEDIATE

Design by Anita Closic

Finished Felted Size
Approx 4-inch diameter

Materials
- Plymouth Galway Worsted 100 percent wool medium weight yarn (210 yds/100g per ball): 1 ball each red #16 (A) and green #82 (B)
- Size 15 (10mm) straight needles
- Tapestry needle
- Small round gold Christmas ornament for center (optional)

Pre-Felted Gauge
10 sts and 13 rows = 4 inches/10cm in St st using 2 strands yarn held tog
Exact gauge is not critical; make sure your sts are loose and airy.

Pattern Notes
1 ball makes 2 roses.
Work with 2 strands held tog throughout.

Rose
With 2 strands A held tog, cast on 59 sts.
Work 12 rows in St st.
  Cut yarn, leaving a 24-inch tail.
  Using tapestry needle, thread tail through all sts and pull tight, gathering rose into a spiral shape.
  Tack center inside bud and bottom edge to secure.
  Weave in all ends.

Leaves
Make 2 or 3
With 2 strands B held tog, cast on 3 sts.
Row 1 (RS): Knit.
Row 2 and all WS rows: Purl.

Row 3: K1, yo, k1, yo, k1. (5 sts)
Row 5: K2, yo, k1, yo, k2. (7 sts)
Row 7: K3, yo, k1, yo, k3. (9 sts)
Row 9: K4, yo, k1, yo, k4. (11 sts)
Row 11: Knit.
Rows 13, 15, 17, 19: Ssk, knit to last 2 sts, k2tog. (3 sts)
Row 21: K3tog. (1 st)
  Cut yarn and fasten off.

Weave in all ends.
  Attach 2 or 3 leaves to base of rose.
  Follow basic felting instructions on page 172 until finished measurements are obtained or rose is desired size.
  After felting, use needle to open up holes in leaves.
  Let dry thoroughly.
  Optional: Place small gold ornament in center. ❄

Accessorize Your Snowman

Enjoy dressing a snowman in his knitted woolens while you can, before he melts away!

Designs by Kathy Sasser

Hat

Finished Size
5½ inches tall

Materials
- Plymouth Encore Worsted 75 percent acrylic/25 percent wool medium weight yarn (200 yds/100g per ball): 1 ball each red #1386 (A), green #54 (B) and black #217 (C)
- Size 6 (4mm) straight and double-pointed (set of 4) or size needed to obtain gauge
- Tapestry needle
- 4–5 plastic grocery bags for blocking

Gauge
20 sts and 27 rows = 4 inches/10cm in St st
To save time, take time to check gauge.

Special Abbreviations
N1, N2, N3: Needle 1, Needle 2, Needle 3
Inc (Increase): Inc 1 by knitting in front and back of st.

Special Technique
3-st I-Cord: Cast on 3 sts. *K3, do not turn, sl sts back to LH needle; rep from * until cord is desired length. Bind off.

Pattern Note
The body of the hat is worked sideways, then seamed; the top is picked up from 1 side of tube, and the brim is picked up from the other side.

Body
With straight needles, cast on 30 sts and work in St st until piece measures 15 inches.
Bind off.
Sew cast-on edge to bound-off edge to form a tube.

Top
With RS facing and using dpns, pick up and knit 78 sts around 1 side of tube.
Distribute sts evenly on 3 dpns (26 on each needle); join and place marker between first and last sts.
Rnd 1: Knit.
Rnd 2: N1: *K1, ssk, knit to last 3 sts, k2tog, k1; rep from * on N2 and N3. (72 sts)
Rep [Rnds 1 and 2] 4 times. (48 sts)
Rep [Rnd 2] 4 times. (24 sts)
Cut yarn, leaving a 6-inch tail.
Using tapestry needle, thread tail through rem sts, and pull tight.

Brim
With RS facing and using dpns, pick up and knit 78 sts around other side of tube.

Distribute sts evenly on 3 dpns (26 on each needle); join and place marker between first and last sts.

Rnd 1: Knit.

Rnd 2: N1: *Inc 3 sts evenly across needle; rep from * for N2 and N3. (87 sts)

Rep [Rnds 1 and 2] 4 times. (123 sts)

Bind off very loosely.

Flower

With A, make I-cord 11 inches long.

Fold cord to make 5 loops and sew tog at center, then attach to hat as shown in photo.

Stem

With B, make I-cord 2½ inches long.

Leaves

Make 2

With B, make I-cord 1½ inches long.

Attach stem and leaves to hat as shown in photo.

Weave in all loose ends and shape hat.

Fill hat with plastic bags; wet and block brim.

Snowman's Scarf

Finished Size

Approx 6 x 52¾ inches

Materials

- Plymouth Encore Worsted 75 percent acrylic/25 percent wool medium weight yarn (200 yds/100g per ball): 2 balls red #1386
- Size 7 (4.5mm) straight needles or size needed to obtain gauge
- Tapestry needle

Gauge

20 sts and 28 rows = 4 inches/10cm in pattern

To save time, take time to check gauge.

Scarf

Cast on 30 sts, placing markers after first 2 sts and before last 2 sts.

Keeping 4 sts at each side in garter st, work center 22 sts as follows:

Rows 1–5: Knit.

Rows 6, 8, 10 and 12: *K2tog, k2, [inc] twice, k3, ssk; rep from *.

Rows 7, 9 and 11: Purl.

Rep these 12 rows until scarf measures approximately 52 inches from beg, or to desired length.

Knit 5 rows and bind off.

I-Cord Fringe

*With RS facing, pick up first 3 sts along cast-on edge. Work I-cord for 5 inches.

Rep from * on next 3 sts on cast-on edge.

Continue to work I-cord fringes along cast-on and bound-off edges.

Tie I-cord ends with a knot.

Weave in all ends.

Carrot Nose

Finished Size

5½ inches long

Materials

- Plymouth Encore Worsted 75 percent acrylic/25 percent wool medium weight yarn (200 yds/100g per ball): 1 ball each orange #1383 (A) and green #54 (B)
- Size 4 (3.5mm) straight needles
- Size 6 (4mm) straight needles or size needed to obtain gauge
- Tapestry needle
- Plastic grocery bag for stuffing

Gauge

20 sts and 22 rows = 4 inches/10cm in garter st with larger needles

To save time, take time to check gauge.

Special Technique

3-st I-Cord: Cast on 3 sts. *K3, do not turn, sl sts back to LH needle; rep from * until cord is desired length. Bind off.

Carrot

With larger needles and A, cast on 3 sts.

Row 1: Knit.

Row 2: Inc, knit across to last st, inc. (5 sts)

Rep last 2 rows until there are 21 sts.

Work 35 rows even.

Next row: Dec 9 sts evenly across row. (12 sts)

Next row: Knit.

Cut yarn, leaving a 10-inch tail.

Using tapestry needle, thread tail through rem sts, and pull tight.

Sew side seam down to end of inc. Stuff carrot with 1 plastic grocery bag, then sew rem opening closed.

Carrot Tops

*With smaller needles and B, pick up 2 sts along top edge. Work 2-st I-cord for 2 inches.

Bind off.

Rep from * making desired number of tops.

Weave in ends.

Gently steam carrot into shape. ❋

Felted Puppet Friends

Any kid will have fun with these Gingerbread Man and Snowman puppets.

Designs by Julie Gaddy

Finished Felted Measurements

8 inches tall x 7½ inches wide (at arms) Measurements achieved using yarn and colors specified; results may vary depending on yarn, yarn color and felting time.

Materials

• Plymouth Galway Chunky 100 percent wool bulky weight yarn (123 yds/100g per ball): 1 ball each brown heather #712 (MC/Gingerbread Man) or off-white #1 (MC/Snowman) and red #16 (CC/ both); small amount black #9

• Medium weight yarn: small amount blue and orange

• Size 13 (9mm) straight needles or size needed to obtain gauge
• Tapestry needle
• Sharp large-eye needle for embroidery

Pre-Felted Gauge

11 sts and 14 rows= 4 inches/10cm in St st
Exact gauge is not critical; make sure your sts are loose and airy.

Special Abbreviation

Inc (Increase): Inc 1 by knitting in front and back of st.

Pattern Notes

Right and left refer to right and left sides of puppet body pieces when looking at the front side.

If making both puppets, felt separately.

All embellishments are added after felted puppet is completely dry.

Gingerbread Man Puppet

Make 2 pieces (front & back)

Lower Body

With MC, cast on 18 sts.
Rows 1 and 3 (WS): Purl.
Row 2: Knit.
Row 4: K1, ssk, knit to last 3 sts, k2tog, k1. (16 sts)
Rep [Rows 1–4] twice. (12 sts)

Vest

Change to CC, and rep Rows 1–4. (10 sts)
Work even in St st for 8 rows.

Shape Head

Change to MC.
Next row (WS): Purl.
Inc row: K1, inc, knit to last 2 sts, inc, k1. (12 sts)
Rep [last 2 rows] twice. (16 sts)
Work 2 rows in St st.

Next row: Purl.

Dec row: K1, ssk, knit to last 3 sts, k2tog, k1. (14 sts)

Rep last 2 rows until 8 sts rem.

Bind off purlwise on WS.

Right Arm

With RS facing and MC, beg 8 rows below head shaping on RH side, pick up and knit 8 sts to head shaping.

Row 1 and all WS rows: Purl.

Row 2: K1, inc, k3, k2tog, k1. (8 sts)

Rows 4, 6, 8: K1, ssk, knit to end. (5 sts)

Row 10: K1, sk2p, k1. (3 sts)

Bind off purlwise on WS.

Left Arm

With RS facing and using MC, beg at last row of vest on left-hand side, pick up and knit 8 sts, ending 8 rows below head shaping.

Row 1 and all WS rows: Purl.

Row 2: K1, ssk, k3, inc, k1. (8 sts)

Rows 4, 6, 8: Knit to last 3 sts, k2tog, k1. (5 sts)

Row 10: K1, sk2p, k1. (3 sts)

Bind off purlwise on WS.

Finishing

Sew front and back of puppet tog. Weave in all ends.

Follow basic felting instructions on page 172 until finished measurements are obtained or puppet is desired size.

Shape and lay flat to dry.

Embellishments

Referring to Fig. 1 for placement, embroider eyes with blue and mouth with red.

With bulky weight off-white yarn, embroider zigzag "icing" around outside edge of entire front of puppet .

Snowman Puppet

Work same as for Gingerbread Man using MC for entire puppet.

Referring to Fig. 2 for placement, embroider eyes with black, carrot nose with orange and mouth with black.

With bulky black yarn, make 3 French knots in center of front between arms for "buttons."

Scarf

With CC, cast on 4 sts.

I-cord: *K4, do not turn, sl sts back to LH needle; rep from * until cord measures 21 inches.

Cut yarn, leaving a 5-inch tail.

Using tapestry needle, thread tail through sts, and pull tight.

Weave in all ends.

Make a knot in each end of scarf and tie scarf around Snowman's neck. Tack in place if desired. ❄

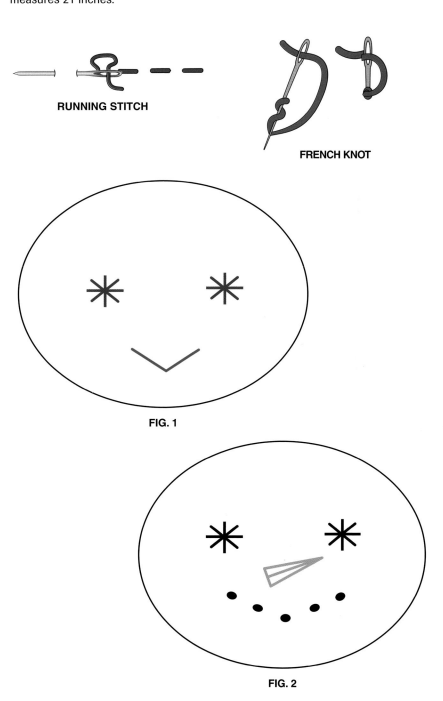

RUNNING STITCH

FRENCH KNOT

FIG. 1

FIG. 2

Sweaters for Santa's Lap

You won't be able to resist these cute holiday sweaters for babies, toddlers and kids (that still "believe"). These fashions are sized from infant to size 8 and make great gifts.

Snowflakes Hoodie

When the snow flies, bundle up your child in this wintry hoodie.

■■■□ INTERMEDIATE

Design by Scarlet Taylor

Sizes
Child's 2 (4, 6, 8)
Instructions are given for smallest size, with larger sizes in parentheses. When only 1 number is given, it applies to all sizes.

Finished Measurements
Chest: 26½ (28, 30, 31) inches
Length: 13¾ (14, 16, 18) inches

Materials
- Plymouth Galway Worsted 100 percent wool medium weight yarn (210 yds/100g per ball): 3 (3, 4, 5) balls pink #135 (A) and 1 (1, 1, 2) ball(s) off-white #1 (B)
- Size 6 (4.25mm) straight needles
- Size 8 (5mm) straight needles or size needed to obtain gauge
- Stitch markers
- 11 (11, 13, 15)-inch separating zipper
- Tapestry needle

Gauge
20 sts and 28 rows = 4 inches/10cm in St st with larger needles
To save time, take time to check gauge.

Special Abbreviation
M1 (Make 1): Insert LH needle from front to back under the horizontal strand between the last st worked and next st on LH needle. With RH needle, knit into the back of this loop.

Pattern Stitch

2-Color K2, P2 Rib (multiple of 4 sts + 2)

Row 1 (RS): K2 B, *p2 A, k2 B; rep from * across.

Row 2: P2 B, *k2 A, p2 B; rep from * across.

Rep Rows 1 and 2 for pat.

Pattern Notes

When working 2-Color K2, P2 Rib, strand color not in use loosely across on WS.

When working Snowflake motif, use Intarsia method, using separate lengths of yarn for each colored section; bring new color up from under old color to lock them.

When measuring for length, allow St st edge to roll.

Hoodie
Back

With smaller needles and A, cast on 66 (70, 74, 78) sts.

Work in St st for approx 1 inch, ending with a WS row.

Change to larger needles, and work 2-Color K2, P2 Rib for approx 1 inch, ending with a WS row. Cut B.

With A only, work in St st until piece measures 8¼ (8, 9½, 11) inches from beg, ending with a WS row.

Shape Armholes

Bind off 5 (5, 7, 7) sts at beg of next 2 rows. (56, 60, 60, 64 sts)

Continue in St st until armholes measure 5½ (6, 6½, 7) inches, ending with a WS row.

Bind off.

Left Front

With smaller needles and A, cast on 34 (34, 38, 38) sts.

Work in St st for approx 1 inch, ending with a WS row.

Change to larger needles, and work 2-Color K2, P2 Rib for approx 1 inch, ending with a WS row. Cut B.

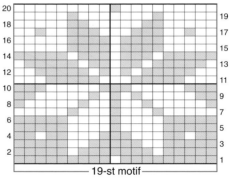

19-st motif

SNOWFLAKES HOODIE

COLOR KEY
- ▨ Pink (A)
- ☐ Off-white (B)

Next row: With A only, knit across, inc 1 st. (35, 35, 39, 39 sts)

Continue in St st until piece measures 6¾ (6½, 8, 9½) inches from beg (allowing edge to roll), ending with a WS row.

Set up pat: K8 (8, 10, 10), place marker, work Row 1 of Snowflake motif from chart, place marker, k8 (8, 10, 10).

Continue working motif between markers until Row 10 of chart has been completed.

Shape Armhole

Next row (RS): With A, bind off 5 (5, 7, 7) sts; cut A, join B, and continue in pats to end of row. (30, 30, 32, 32 sts)

Work even until Row 20 of chart has been completed. Cut A.

Continue in B only, and work even until armhole measures 3¾ (4, 4½, 5) inches, ending with a RS row.

Shape Neck

Next row (WS): P9 (8, 10, 9) sts and place these sts on holder for hood; purl to end of row. (21, 22, 22, 23 sts)

Dec row (RS): Knit to last 3 sts, k2tog, k1.

Continue in St st and rep Dec row [every other row] 4 times. (16, 17, 17, 18 sts)

Work even until armhole measures same as back, ending with a WS row.

Bind off.

Right Front

Work same as for left front to armhole shaping, ending with Row 9 of chart.

Shape Armhole

With A, bind off 5 (5, 7, 7) sts, continue in pats to end of row. (30, 30, 32, 32 sts)

Cut A.

Next row (RS): With B, continue as for Left Front to neck shaping, ending with a WS row.

Shape Neck

Next row (RS): K9 (8, 10, 9) and place these sts on holder for hood; knit to end of row. Work 1 row even on rem 21 (22, 22, 23) sts.

Dec row (RS): K1, ssk, knit to end of row. (20, 21, 21, 22 sts)

Rep Dec row [every other row] 4 times. (16, 17, 17, 18 sts)

Continue as for Left Front.

Sleeves

With smaller needles and A, cast on 34 (34, 38, 42) sts.

Work in St st for approx 1 inch, ending with a WS row.

Change to larger needles, and work 2-Color K2, P2 Rib for approx 1 inch, ending with a WS row. Cut B.

With A, work 6 (4, 4, 6) rows even in St st.

Inc row (RS): K1, M1, knit to last st, M1, k1. (36, 36, 40, 44 sts)

Continue in St st and rep Inc row [every 4th row] 0 (1, 0, 0) times, then [every 6th row] 6 (11, 12, 12) times, then [every 8th] 3 (0, 0, 1) times. (54, 60, 64, 70 sts)

Work even until sleeve measures 12½ (13¾, 14½, 15½) inches from beg, ending with a WS row.

Bind off.

Finishing

Block pieces to measurements.

Sew shoulder seams.

Hood

With RS facing, using larger needles and A, pick up and knit 68 (70, 70, 72) sts around neck edge, including sts from holders.

Work 5 rows in St st, beg with a purl row.

Next row (RS): K7 (8, 8, 9), M1, [k6, M1] 9 times, k7 (8, 8, 9). (78, 80, 80, 82 sts) Work even for 5 rows.

Next row (RS): [K7, M1] 10 times, k8 (10, 10, 12). (88, 90, 90, 92 sts)

Work even until hood measures approx 10½ (11½, 12½, 12½) inches from beg, ending with a WS row.

Bind off.

With right sides tog, fold in half and sew bound-off edge tog for top.

Right Front & Right Half of Hood Bands

With RS facing, using smaller needles and A, beg above rolled edge, pick up and knit 55 (55, 65, 75) sts evenly along right front edge to beg of hood, place marker, continue to pick up and knit 54 (58, 62, 62) sts evenly along right half of hood, ending at top center. (109, 113, 127, 137 sts)

Next row: Knit to 6 sts before marker, [yo, ktog] for hole for drawstring, knit to end.

Knit 1 row.

Next row: Knit to marker, join a 2nd

ball of yarn and bind off front band sts.

Continuing on hood sts, knit 4 rows for hem.

Bind off.

Left Front & Left Half of Hood Bands

Work as for right front bands, beg at top center of hood, placing marker same as for right front, and end at lower edge of left front. Make hole opposite hole on right half of hood. Continue as for right front, binding off front edge sts first, then continuing on hood sts.

Sew in sleeves. Sew side and underarm seams.

Join side edges of right and left hood bands at top center.

Twisted Cord

Cut 1 strand each of A and B approx 13 (14, 14, 14½) feet. Fold in half and secure folded end to a stationary object (like a doorknob). Twist yarn until it begins to double back on itself. Fold in half again with both ends tog and allow to twist upon itself. Cut to 27 (28, 28, 29) inches or desired length and knot the ends to secure.

Place cord inside hood hem, and pull each end through holes. Fold hem to WS and sew in place.

Pompoms

With A, make 2 (2-inch) pompoms as follows:

Cut 2 cardboard circles 2-inches in diameter. Cut a hole in the center of each circle, about ½ inch in diameter. Thread a tapestry needle with a length of A doubled. Holding both circles tog, insert needle through center hole, over the outside edge, through center again until entire circle is covered and center hole is filled (thread more length of yarn as needed).

With sharp scissors, cut yarn between the 2 circles all around the circumference. Using 2 (12-inch) strands of A, slip yarn between circles and overlap yarn ends 2 or 3 times to prevent knot from slipping, pull tightly and tie into a firm knot. Remove cardboard and fluff out pompom by rolling it between your hands. Trim even with scissors. Attach 1 pompom to each end of cord.

Sew in zipper.

Weave in ends. ❋

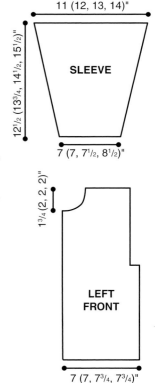

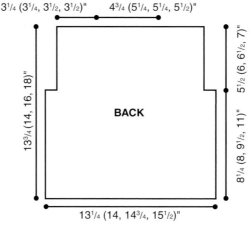

Cable Your Wishes Pullover

This shawl-collared pullover is just the thing for frosty days.

Design by Kristin Omdahl

Sizes

Child's 2 (4, 6, 8, 10) Instructions are given for smallest size, with larger sizes in parentheses. When only 1 number is given, it applies to all sizes.

Finished Measurements

Chest: 23½ (25½, 27½, 28½, 30½) inches
Length: 12 (15¼, 15½, 17½, 19½) inches

Materials

- Plymouth Country 8 Ply 100 percent superwash wool light weight yarn (105 yds/50g per ball): 4 (5, 6, 7, 7) balls teal #2268
- Size 7 (4.5mm) straight and 24-inch circular needles or size needed to obtain gauge
- Cable needle
- Stitch markers 2 in CC
- Tapestry needle

Gauge

20 sts and 24 rows = 4 inches/10cm in K4, P4 Rib
To save time, take time to check gauge.

Special Abbreviations

C8B (Cable 8 Back): Sl 4 sts to cn and hold in back, k4, k4 from cn.
C4F (Cable 4 Front): Sl 2 sts to cn and hold in front, k2, k2 from cn.

M1 (Make 1): Insert LH needle from front to back under the horizontal strand between the last st worked and next st on left needle. With RH needle, knit into the back of this loop.

Special Technique

Wrap and turn: Sl next st, (wyif if last st was knit, or wyib if last st was purled), bring the yarn to back (or front). Place marker on the LH needle and return the slipped st to the LH needle.

Pattern Stitch

Cable (16-st panel)

Rows 1 and all WS rows: Purl.

Rows 2 and 4 (RS): Knit.

Row 6: [C8B] twice.

Rows 8 and 10: Knit.

Row 12: [K2, C4F, k2] twice.

Rep Rows 1–12 for pat.

Pattern Notes

The shawl collar is worked using short rows. Read instructions carefully.

Pullover

Back

Cast on 54 (62, 66, 70, 74) sts.

Set up rib (RS): K2, *p2, k2; rep from * across.

Work 1½ (2, 2, 2, 2) inches in rib as established, ending with a RS row and inc 8 (6, 6, 6, 6) sts evenly across on last row. (62, 68, 72, 76, 80 sts)

Set up rib and Cable (WS): *P3 (0, 0, 2, 0), k4 (2, 4, 4, 0), [p4, k4] 2 (3, 3, 3, 4) times, place marker, work Cable pat over next 16 sts, place marker, [k4, p4] 2 (3, 3, 3, 4) times, k4 (2, 4, 4, 0), p3 (0, 0, 2, 0).

Continue working ribs and Cable pat as established until piece measures approx 7 (7, 9, 10½, 11¾) inches, ending with a WS row.

Raglan Shaping

Bind off 6 sts at beg of next 2 rows. (50, 56, 60, 64, 68 sts)

Dec row (RS): K1, k2tog, work in pats as established to last 3 sts, ssk, k1. Continue in pats as established and rep Dec row [every other row] 14 (17, 18, 20, 22) times. (20, 20, 22, 22, 22 sts)

Bind off.

Front

Work as for back (including all shaping) until piece measures approx 9 (9½, 11¼, 12¾, 14½) inches, ending with a WS row.

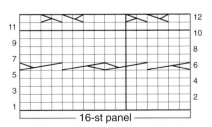

16-st panel

CABLE YOUR WISHES PULLOVER

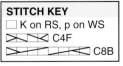

STITCH KEY

☐ K on RS, p on WS

C4F

C8B

Placket Opening

Next row (RS): Work to center 8 sts, attach a 2nd ball of yarn, bind off center 8 sts, work to end of row.

Working both sides at once, continue in pat and raglan shaping until piece measures approx 10¾ (14, 14, 16, 18) inches.

Neck Shaping

Working both sides at once, continue raglan shaping and *at the same time,* bind off 2 (2, 3, 3, 3) sts at each neck edge.

Dec row (RS): Continuing raglan shaping, work to 3 sts before left neck edge, k2tog, k1; on right neck edge k1, ssk, work to end of row.

Rep Dec row [every other row] 2 (2, 3, 3, 3) times. Complete raglan shaping and fasten off last st.

Bind off.

Sleeves
Cuff

Cast on 30 (34, 34, 38, 38) sts.

Set up rib (RS): K2, *p2, k2; rep from * across.

Work even in rib as established for approx 1½ (1½, 2, 2, 2,) inches, ending on a WS row and inc 2 (2, 4, 2, 4) sts evenly across on last row. (32, 36, 38, 40, 42 sts)

Sleeve Shaping

Set up rib (RS): K2 (3, 4, 5, 1), *p4, k4; rep from * to last 6 (7, 8, 9, 5) sts, end p4, k2 (3, 4, 5, 1).

Work even in rib as established for 5 (3, 5, 5, 5) rows.

Inc row (RS): K1, M1, work in pat as established to last st, M1, k1.

Rep Inc row [every 6 rows] 2 (7, 8, 6, 6) times, then [every 8 (0, 0, 8, 8) rows] 1 (0, 0, 2, 3) time(s), working new sts in rib as established. (40, 52, 56, 58, 62 sts)

Work even until piece measures 7 (10½, 12, 12½, 14) inches, ending with a WS row.

Cap Shaping

Bind off 6 sts at beg of next 2 rows. (28, 40, 44, 46, 50 sts)

Dec row (RS): K1, k2tog, work in rib to last 3 sts, ssk, k1. (26, 38, 42, 44, 48 sts)

Continue in rib and rep Dec row [every other row] 6 (15, 18, 18, 20) times, then [every 4th row] 4 (1, 0, 1, 1) time(s). (6 sts rem)

Bind off.

Finishing

Block pieces to measurements.

Sew raglan, underarm, and side seams.

Placket & Shawl Collar

With RS facing and using circular needle, pick up and knit 12 (18, 18, 19, 21) sts along placket edge, place marker for neck, pick up and knit 10 (10, 12, 12, 12) sts along front neck, place turning marker in CC, pick up and knit 18 (18, 20, 20, 20) sts along back neck st, place turning marker (CC), pick up and knit 10 (10, 12, 12, 12) sts along front neck, place marker for neck, pick up and knit 12 (18, 18, 19, 21) st along placket edge. (62, 74, 80, 82, 86 sts) Working in St st, work short rows as follows: work to 2nd turning marker, remove marker, Wrap and Turn. *Work back to opposite marker, remove marker, Wrap and Turn. Rep from * until all sts between neck markers are worked.

Turn and continue working all sts on needle, hiding wraps by working them tog with wrapped st as k2tog (or p2tog if working WS row).

Work even until placket bands measure approx ½ inch, or just short of width of placket opening.

Work 4 rows in garter st, then bind off knitwise.

Overlap bands by sewing 1 edge of band to bound-off sts of placket opening, then tacking other edge of band to same bound-off sts on inside.

Weave in all ends. ❆

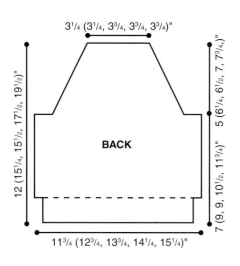

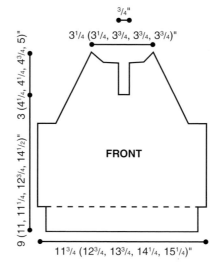

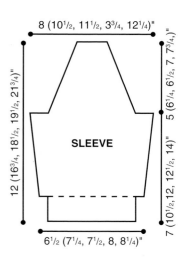

Gift-Wrapped Cardigan & Headband

Wrap your little girl in festive colors and a trendy style for the holidays!

Designs by Scarlet Taylor

Sizes

Child's 2 (4, 6, 8) Instructions are given for smallest size, with larger sizes in parentheses. When only 1 number is given, it applies to all sizes.

Finished Measurements

Chest: 24 (26½, 27, 28) inches
Length: 12½ (13, 14, 15) inches

Materials

- Plymouth Country Prints 8 Ply 100 percent superwash wool light weight yarn (105 yds/50g per ball): 6 (7, 7, 8) balls crayon-multi #9
- One size 6 (4mm) straight needles
- One size 7 (4.5mm) straight needles or size needed to obtain gauge
- ⅝-inch-wide red grosgrain ribbon approx 54 inches long
- Stitch marker
- Tapestry needle

Gauge

20 sts and 28 rows = 4 inches/10cm in St st with larger needles
To save time, take time to check gauge.

Special Abbreviation

M1 (Make 1): Insert LH needle from front to back under the horizontal strand between the last st worked and next st on left needle. With RH needle, knit into the back of this loop.

Pattern Stitch

Seed St (even number sts)

Row 1 (RS): *K1, p1; rep from * across.
Row 2: *P1, k1; rep from * across.
Rep Rows 1 and 2 for pat.

Pattern Note

Carefully read through instructions before shaping fronts.

Cardigan
Back

With smaller needles, cast on 52 (58, 60, 62) sts.

Work in Seed St for 1 inch, ending with a WS row.

Change to larger needles and work 8 (8, 8, 10) rows in St st.

Shape Waist

Inc row (RS): K2, M1, knit to last 2 sts, M1, k2.

Continue in St st and rep Inc row [every 8 (8, 8,10) rows] 3 times. (60, 66, 68, 70 sts)

Work even until piece measures 6 (6, 6½, 7¼) inches from beg, ending with a WS row.

Shape Armholes

Bind off 3 sts at beg of next 2 rows. (54, 60, 62, 64 sts)

Work even in St st until armhole measures 5½ (6, 6½, 6¾) inches, ending with a WS row.

Shape Shoulders

Bind off 8 (9, 10, 10) sts at beg of next 2 rows, then 8 (9, 9, 9) sts at beg of

following 2 rows. (22, 24, 24, 26 sts)
Bind off for back neck.

Right Front

With smaller needles, cast on 50 (52, 56, 58) sts.

Work in Seed St for approx 1 inch, ending with a WS row.

Change to larger needles.

Next row (RS): Work 5 sts in Seed St for band, place marker, knit to end of row.

Next row: Purl to marker, work 5 sts in Seed St.

Shape Front

Continue in pats as established and work waist inc as for back at side edge only.

At the same time, dec for front slope as follows:

Dec row (RS): Work to marker, ssk, knit to end of row. (49, 51, 55, 57 sts)

Rep Dec row [every other row] 34 (32, 35, 35) times, then every 4th row 0 (2, 2, 4) times, and *at the same time* when piece measures same as back to armhole, bind off 3 sts at armhole edge.

After all shaping is complete, work even on rem 16 (18, 19, 19) sts until piece measures same as back to shoulder shaping, ending with a RS row.

Shape Shoulder

Bind off 8 (9, 10, 10) sts at beg of next row.

Work 1 row even, then bind off rem 8 (9, 9, 9) sts at shoulder edge.

Left Front

With smaller needles, cast on 50 (52, 56, 58) sts.

Work in Seed St for approx 1 inch, ending with a RS row.

Change to larger needles.

Next row (WS): Work 5 sts in Seed St for band, place marker, work in St st to end of row.

Shape Front

Continue in pats as established and work waist inc as for back at side edge only.

At same the time, dec for front slope as follows:

Dec row (RS): Work to 2 sts before marker, k2tog, sl marker and work in Seed St to end of row. (49, 51, 55, 57 sts)

Rep Dec row [every other row] 34 (32, 35, 35) times, then [every 4th row] 0 (2, 2, 4) times, *and at the same time* when piece measures same as back to armhole, bind off 3 sts at armhole edge.

After all shaping is complete, work even on rem 16 (18, 19, 19) sts until piece measures same as back to shoulder shaping, ending with a WS row.

Shape shoulder same as for right front.

Sleeves

With smaller needles, cast on 32 (38, 38, 40) sts.

Work in Seed St for approx 1 inch, ending with a WS row.

Change to larger needles and work 6 rows in St st.

Inc row (RS): K1, M1, knit to last st, M1, k1. (34, 40, 40, 42 sts)

Continue in St st, and rep Inc row [every 6th row] 8 (4, 10, 10) times, then [every 8th row] 2 (6, 2, 3) times. (54, 60, 64, 68 sts)

Work even until sleeve measures 12½ (13¾, 14¼, 15½) inches from beg, ending with a WS row.

Bind off.

Finishing

Block pieces to measurements.

Sew shoulder seams.

With RS facing and smaller needles, pick up and knit 24 (27, 27, 28) sts along back neck. Bind off knitwise.

Sew in sleeves.

Sew right-side seam, leaving a ¾-inch opening ½ inch above cast-on edge to pull ribbon through.

Sew left side and underarm seams.

Weave in ends.

Sew end of 30-inch length of ribbon to WS of left front edge. Sew end of 24-inch length of ribbon to WS of right front edge. Trim for best fit.

Headband

With larger needles, cast on 12 sts.

Work in Seed St until headband measures approx 18 (20, 20½, 21) inches or desired length when slightly stretched.

Bind off.

Sew edges tog. ❆

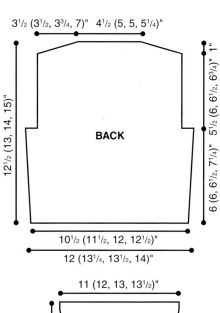

3½ (3½, 3¾, 7)"   4½ (5, 5, 5¼)"

12½ (13, 14, 15)"

6 (6, 6½, 7¼)"   5½ (6, 6½, 6¾)"   1"

BACK

10½ (11½, 12, 12½)"

12 (13¼, 13½, 14)"

11 (12, 13, 13½)"

12½ (13¾, 14¼, 15½)"

SLEEVE

6½ (7½, 7½, 8)"

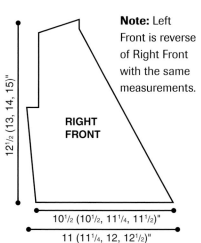

Note: Left Front is reverse of Right Front with the same measurements.

12½ (13, 14, 15)"

RIGHT FRONT

10½ (10½, 11¼, 11½)"

11 (11¼, 12, 12½)"

Cable-Rib Vest

Every small lad needs a special holiday vest this Christmas season!

◼◼◻◻ EASY

Design by Sara Louise Harper

Sizes

Child's 6 months (12 months, 2, 4, 6, 8) Instructions are given for smallest size, with larger sizes in parentheses. When only 1 number is given, it applies to all sizes.

Finished Measurements

Chest: 21 (22, 24, 26, 28, 30) inches
Length: 11 (12, 14, 15, 16, 17) inches

Materials

- Plymouth Country 8 Ply 100 percent superwash light weight wool (105 yds/50g per ball): 2 balls red #2232 (MC) and 2 (2, 3, 3, 3, 3) balls green #2276 (CC)
- Size 7 (4.5mm) straight and 16-inch circular needles or size needed to obtain gauge
- Cable needle
- Stitch markers
- Tapestry needle

Gauge

22 sts and 24 rows = 4 inches/10cm in Christmas Rib pat (blocked)
To save time, take time to check gauge.

Special Abbreviations

RC (Right Cross): Sl 2 sts to cn and hold in back, k1, k2 from cn.
LC (Left Cross): Sl 1 st to cn and hold in front, k2, k1 from cn.

Pattern Stitches

A. K2, P2 Rib (multiple of 4 sts + 2)
Row 1 (RS): K2, *p2, k2; rep from * across row.
Row 2: P2, *k2, p2; rep from * across row.

Rep Rows 1 and 2 for pat.
B. Christmas Rib (multiple of 8 sts + 2)
Row 1 (WS): With MC, k2, *p6, k2; rep from * across.
Row 2: With MC, p2, *sl 1, k4, sl 1, p2; rep from * across.
Rows 3 and 5: With CC, k2, *sl 1, p4, sl 1, k2; rep from * across.
Row 4: With CC, rep Row 2.
Row 6: With CC, p2, *LC, RC, p2; rep from * across.
Rep Rows 1–6 for pat.

Pattern Notes

Work all dec 1 st from edge; work ssk at right edge and k2tog at left edge.

This st pat pulls in and must be blocked.

Vest

Back

Using MC, cast on 54 (58, 66, 70, 78, 82) sts.

Work 6 rows in K2, P2 Rib.

Change to CC and work 7 rows in St st.

Next row (WS): With MC, k2 (0, 0, 2, 2,

0), work in Christmas Rib to last 2 (0, 0, 2, 2, 0) sts, k2 (0, 0, 2, 2, 0).

Work even in pats as established (working first and last 2 sts in rev St st for sizes 6 months, 4 and 6 only) until piece measures 6 (6½, 8, 9, 9½, 10) inches from beg, ending with a WS row.

Shape Armholes
Bind off 5 sts at beg of next 2 rows. (44, 48, 56, 60, 68, 72 sts)

Continue in pat as established and dec 1 st at each armhole edge on next row, then [every other row] twice. (38, 42, 50, 54, 62, 66 sts)

Work even until armhole measures 5 (5½, 6, 6, 6½, 7) inches, ending with a WS row.

Bind off.

Front
Work as for back to armhole shaping.

Shape Armholes & V-Neck
Next row (RS): Bind off 5 sts (1 st rem on RH needle), work in pat for 20 (22, 26, 28, 32, 34) sts, attach a 2nd ball of yarn and bind off center 2 sts, work in pat to end.

Continue to shape armholes as for back and *at the same time,* dec 1 st at each neck edge [every RS row] 14 (14, 15, 15, 17, 20) times. (5, 7, 8, 11, 12, 12 sts)

Work even until front measures same as back.

Bind off.

Finishing
Block pieces to measurements.
Sew shoulder and side seams.

V-Neck Edge
With circular needle and MC, beg at left shoulder, pick up and knit 24 (26, 28, 28, 30, 32) sts along left neck, place marker, pick up and knit 2 sts in front V, place marker, pick up and knit 24 (26, 28, 28, 30, 32) along front neck and 26 (26, 30, 30, 34, 38) across back neck;

join and place marker for beg of rnd. (76, 80, 88, 88, 96, 104 sts)

Rnd 1: P0 (2, 0, 0, 2, 0), *k2, p2; rep from * to last 0 (2, 0, 0, 2, 0) sts, k0 (2, 0, 0, 2, 0). *Note: Center V should be k2.*

Work 2 rnds in K2, P2 Rib as established.

Dec rnd 1: Work in rib as established to 2 sts before marker, p2tog, k2, p2tog, work in rib to end of rnd.

Dec rnd 2: Work in rib to 3 sts before

marker, ssk, p1, k2, p1, k2tog, work in rib to end of rnd.

Bind off in pat.

Armhole Edges
With circular needle and MC, pick up and knit 48 (52, 56, 60, 64, 66) sts around armhole.

Work 3 rnds in K2, P2 Rib.
Bind off in pat.
Weave in all ends. ❋

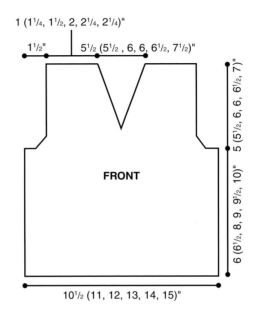

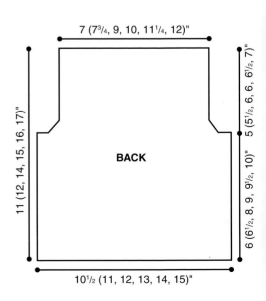

Dots-for-the-Daughters Pullover

This pullover is simple, elegant and perfect for holiday occasions all winter long!

■■□□ EASY

Design by Sara Louise Harper

Sizes

Child's 2 (4, 6, 8) Instructions are given for smallest size, with larger sizes in parentheses. When only 1 number is given, it applies to all sizes.

Finished Measurements

Chest: 24 (26, 28, 30) inches
Length: 14 (15, 16, 17) inches

Materials

- Plymouth Merino Supreme 100 percent merino wool medium weight yarn (64 yds/50g per ball): 9 (10, 12, 15) skeins red #2209
- Size 8 (5mm) 16-inch circular needle
- Size 9 (5.5mm) straight needles or size needed to obtain gauge
- Spare size 9 needle for bind off
- Stitch holders
- Stitch markers
- Tapestry needle

(4 MEDIUM)

Gauge

16 sts and 21 rows = 4 inches/10cm in Textured Dot pat with larger needles
To save time, take time to check gauge.

Special Abbreviation

MK (Make Knot): [P3tog, k3tog, p3tog] in next 3 sts.

Special Technique

3-Needle Bind Off
With RS tog and needles parallel, using a 3rd needle, knit tog a st from the front needle with 1 from the back. *Knit tog a st from the front and back needles, and sl the first st over the 2nd to bind off. Rep from * across, then fasten off last st.

Pattern Stitches

A. Garter Rib (multiple of 6 sts)
Row/Rnd 1: *K3, p3; rep from * across.
Row/Rnd 2 (RS): Knit.
    Rep Rows 1 and 2 for pat.

B. Textured Dot (multiple of 8 sts + 9)
Rows 1, 3, 5, 9, 11 (RS): Knit.
Row 2 and all WS rows: Purl.
Row 7: K3, *MK, k5; rep from * to last 6 sts, MK, k3.
Row 13: K7, *MK, k5; rep from * to last 10 sts, MK, k7.
Row 14: Purl.
    Rep Rows 3–14 for pat.

Pattern Notes

Work sleeve inc 1 st in from edge.
    It is not critical to center Textured Dot pat on sleeve; work all inc in pat as established.

Pullover

Back

With larger needles, cast on 51 (54, 57, 60) sts.
Set up rib (WS): Work in Garter Rib to last 3 (0, 3, 0) sts, k3 (0, 3, 0).
    Continue in Garter Rib for 3 inches, ending on a WS row and on last row, dec 2 (inc 3, 6, 5) st evenly across. (49, 57, 63, 65 sts)

Set up pat (RS): K0 (0, 3, 0), work Textured Dot pat to last 0 (0, 3, 0) sts, k0 (0, 3, 0).

Working 3 edge sts each end in St st on Size 6 only, work even in pat as established until piece measures 13½ (14½, 15½, 16½) inches from beg, ending with a WS row.

Back Neck Shaping

Next row (RS): Work 16 (17, 18, 19) sts in pat, attach 2nd ball of yarn and bind off center 17 (23, 27, 27) sts, work in pat to end of row.

Working both sides at once, work 1 row even, then dec 1 st each neck edge once. (15, 16, 17, 18 sts)

Work 1 row even, then place sts on holders.

Front

Work as for back until piece measures 11½ (12½, 13½, 14½) inches, ending with a WS row.

Front Neck Shaping

Next row (RS): Work 19 (23, 25, 25) sts in pat, attach 2nd ball of yarn and bind off center 11 (11, 13, 15) sts, work in pat to end of row.

Working both sides at once, bind off 2 sts at neck edge [every other row] twice. (15, 19, 21, 21 sts each side)

Dec 1 st at neck edge [every other row] 0 (3, 4, 3) times. (15, 16, 17, 18 sts) Work even until front measures same as back.

Place sts on holders.

Sleeves

With larger needles, cast on 21 (24, 27, 30) sts.

Work in Garter Rib as for back for 2 inches, ending with a WS row.

Begin Textured Dot pat and inc 1 st each side [every 3 (3, 3, 4) rows] 15 (15, 16, 18) times, working new sts in pat as established. (51, 54, 59, 66 sts)

Work even until piece measures 10

(11, 12, 14) inches from beg. Bind off.

Finishing

Block pieces to measurements.

Join the shoulders using 3-needle bind off.

Neckband

With circular needle, pick up and knit 60 (66, 66, 72) sts evenly around neck; join and place marker for beg of rnd.

Work in Garter Rib until neckband measures 2 inches or desired length.

Bind off loosely.

Place markers 6 (6½, 7, 8) inches from top of shoulder on front and back and sew sleeves between markers.

Sew side and underarm seams.

Weave in all ends. ❋

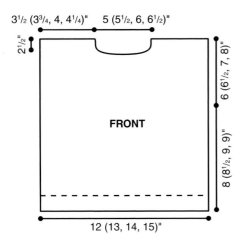

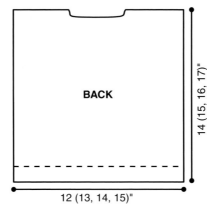

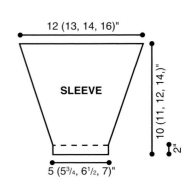

Candy Cane Cropped Cardie

Celebrate sweetness with this tribute to the candy cane!

■■□□ EASY

Design by Sara Louise Harper

Sizes

Child's 6 months (12 months, 2, 4, 6, 8) Instructions are given for smallest size, with larger sizes in parentheses. When only 1 number is given, it applies to all sizes.

Finished Measurements

Chest: 21 (22, 24, 26, 28, 30) inches
Length: 7 (8, 9, 10, 11, 12) inches

Materials

- Plymouth Country 8 Ply 100 percent superwash light weight wool (105 yds/50g per ball): 2 (3, 3, 4, 4, 5) balls red #2232 (MC) and 2 (2, 3, 3, 3, 4) balls cream #2234 (CC)
- Size 7 (4.5mm) straight needles or size needed to obtain gauge
- 1-inch button
- Tapestry needle

Gauge

22 sts and 33 rows = 4 inches/10cm in Candy Cane pat
To save time, take time to check gauge.

Pattern Stitch

Candy Cane Pat (multiple of 8 sts + 6)
Row 1 (RS): With CC, k2, *sl 2, k6; rep from * to last 4 sts, sl 2, k2.
Row 2: With CC, p2, *sl 2, p6; rep from * to last 4 sts, sl 2, p2.
Row 3: With MC, k6, *sl 2, k6; rep from * across.

Row 4: With MC, p6, *sl 2, p6; rep from * across.

Rep Rows 1–4 for pat.

Pattern Notes

When slipping sts, always sl purlwise.

Work sleeve inc 1 st in from edge.

Carry yarns not-in-use up side of work; do not cut.

Cardie
Back

With MC, cast on 58 (60, 66, 72, 76, 82) sts. Knit 4 rows, and on last row, inc 4 (6, 4, 2, 2, 4) sts evenly across. (62, 66, 70, 74, 78, 86 sts)

Working first and last 0 (2, 0, 2, 0, 0) sts in St st, work in Candy Cane Pat until piece measures 7 (8, 9, 10, 11, 12) inches from beg.

Bind off.

Right Front

With MC, cast on 28 (29, 32, 34, 36, 40) sts.

Knit 4 rows, and on last row, inc 0 (1, 0, 0, 0, 0) sts. (28, 30, 32, 34, 36, 40 sts)

Working first and last 3 (0, 1, 2, 3, 1) sts in St st, work in Candy Cane Pat until piece measures 3¾ (4¾, 5¾, 6¾, 7¾, 8¾) inches from beg, ending with a WS row.

Buttonhole row (RS): K2, bind off 2 sts for buttonhole, work in pat to end.

Next row: Cast on 2 sts over the bound-off sts.

Neck Shaping

Next row (RS): Bind off 5 (5, 6, 6, 7, 7) sts, work in pat to end of row.

Work 1 row even.

At beg of next row, bind off 0 (0, 2, 2, 2, 2) sts, then dec 1 st at neck edge [every other row] 6 (7, 6, 7, 6, 7) times. (17, 18, 18, 19, 21, 24 sts)

Work even until piece measures same as back.

Bind off.

Left Front

With MC, cast on 28 (29, 32, 34, 36, 40) sts.

Knit 4 rows, and on last row, inc 0 (1, 0, 0, 0, 0) sts. (28, 30, 32, 34, 36, 40 sts)

Working first and last 3 (0, 1, 2, 3, 1) sts in St st, work in Candy Cane pat until piece measures 4 (5, 6, 7, 8, 9) inches from beg, ending with a RS row.

Neck Shaping

Next row (WS): Bind off 5 (5, 6, 6, 7, 7) sts, work in pat to end of row.

Work 1 row even.

At beg of next row, bind off 0 (0, 2, 2, 2, 2) sts, then dec 1 st at neck edge [every other row] 6 (7, 6, 7, 6, 7) times. (17, 18, 18, 19, 21, 24 sts)

Work even until piece measures same as back.

Bind off.

Sleeves

With MC, cast on 28 (28, 28, 32, 34, 42) sts.

Knit 4 rows.

Change to CC.

Working in St st, alternate CC and MC every 4 rows and *at the same time,* inc 1 st each end [every 3 (3, 3, 3, 4, 4) rows] 11 (14, 14, 14, 15, 16) times. (44, 48, 48, 52, 62, 72 sts)

Work even until sleeve measures 7 (8, 9, 11, 12, 13) inches from beg.

Bind off.

Finishing

Block pieces to measurements.

Sew shoulder seams.

Place markers 5½ (6, 6, 6½, 7, 8) inches down from top of shoulders on fronts and back, then sew sleeves between these markers.

Sew sleeve and side seams.

I-Cord Trim

With CC, cast on 3 sts.

*K3, do not turn, sl sts back to LH needle; rep from * until cord measures 22 (26, 28, 32, 36, 40) inches and place sts on holder.

Sew cord to front, beg at lower right edge and going up right front, across back neck and down left front. (If necessary, work more rows or unravel rows sts to reach lower left front.)

K3tog and fasten off.

Weave in all ends.

Sew button to left front opposite buttonhole. ❋

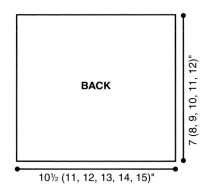

BACK

7 (8, 9, 10, 11, 12)"

10½ (11, 12, 13, 14, 15)"

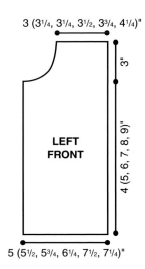

3 (3¼, 3¼, 3½, 3¾, 4¼)"

3"

LEFT FRONT

4 (5, 6, 7, 8, 9)"

5 (5½, 5¾, 6¼, 7½, 7¼)"

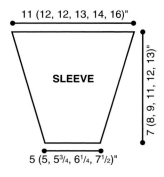

11 (12, 12, 13, 14, 16)"

SLEEVE

7 (8, 9, 11, 12, 13)"

5 (5, 5¾, 6¼, 7½)"

Winter Holiday Throws

We've included afghans to use throughout your home or to give as gifts. Make them in all sizes, from small lap-size to large enough to keep you warm while napping on the sofa.

Holly Days Throw

This heirloom-quality throw will be a treasured holiday addition with its lacy lattice pattern and holly embellishments.

■■■□ INTERMEDIATE

Design by Posey Salem

Finished Size
Approx 45 X 55 inches

Materials
- Plymouth Galway Chunky 100 percent wool bulky weight yarn (123 yds/100g per ball): 15 balls off-white #1 (A) **[5 BULKY]**
- Plymouth Galway Worsted 100 percent wool medium weight yarn (210 yds/100g per ball): 1 ball each red #16 (B) and green #17 (C) **[4 MEDIUM]**
- Size 8 (5mm) straight needles
- Size 10 (6mm) 40-inch circular needle or size needed to obtain gauge
- Stitch markers
- Tapestry needle
- Straight pins
- Sewing needle
- Off-white sewing thread

Gauge
15½ sts and 27 rows = 4 inches/10cm in Seed St with larger needles and A. To save time, take time to check gauge.

Special Abbreviation
Inc (Increase): Inc 1 by knitting in front and back of st.

Pattern Stitches
A. Seed St (odd number of sts)
Row 1: K1, *p1, k1; rep from * to end.
Rep Row 1 for pat.
B. Lattice 'n' Lace (multiple of 8 sts + 3)
Row 1 (RS): K1, *k2tog, k1, yo, k1, ssk, k2; rep from * to last 2 sts, k2.
Row 2 and all WS rows: Purl.

Row 3: *K2tog, k1, [yo, k1] twice, ssk; rep from * to last 3 sts, k3.
Row 5: K2, *yo, k3, yo, k1, ssk, k1; rep from * to last st, k1.
Row 7: K4, *k2tog, k1, yo, k1, ssk, k2; rep from * to last 7 sts, k2tog, k1, yo, k1, ssk, k1.
Row 9: K3, *k2tog, k1, [yo, k1] twice, ssk; rep from * to end.

Row 11: K2, *k2tog, k1, yo, k3, yo, k1; rep from * to last st, k1.
Row 12: Purl.
Rep Rows 1–12 for pat.

Pattern Notes
Afghan is worked back and forth in rows; circular needle is used to accommodate the large number of sts.

The st count of the lace pat increases and decreases on certain rows; sts should be counted after Rows 5, 6, 11 and 12 only.

Throw

Bottom Border

With larger needles and A, cast on 173 sts.

Work in Seed St for 22 rows.

Next row (WS): Work 11 sts in Seed St, purl to last 11 sts inc 4 sts evenly across, work 11 sts in Seed St. (177 sts)

Side Borders & Lattice 'n' Lace Pat

(RS): Work 11 sts in Seed St, place marker, work 18 reps Row 1 of Lattice 'n' Lace, place marker, work 11 sts in Seed St.

Continue in established pat until piece measures 51 inches from beg, ending with a RS row.

Top Border

Next row (WS): Work 11 sts in Seed St, purl to last 11 sts, dec 4 sts evenly across, work 11 sts in Seed St. (173 sts)

Work in Seed St for 23 rows.

Bind off.

Holly Embellishment

Leaves

Make 14

With smaller needles and C, cast on 3 sts.

Row 1 (RS): Inc, k1, inc. (5 sts)

Row 2, 4, 6, 8 (WS): Purl.

Row 3: K2, yo, k1, yo, k2. (7 sts)

Row 5: K3, yo, k1, yo, k3. (9 sts)

Row 7: K4, yo, k1, yo, k4. (11 sts)

Row 9: Bind off 3 sts (1 st rem on RH needle), [k1, yo] twice, k5. (10 sts)

Row 10: Bind off 3 sts, purl to end. (7 sts)

Row 11: K3, yo, k1, yo, k3. (9 sts)

Rows 12 and 14: Purl.

Row 13: K4, yo, k1, yo, k4. (11 sts)

Row 15: Bind off 3 sts, knit to end. (8 sts)

Row 16: Bind off 3 sts, purl to end. (5 sts)

Row 17: Ssk, k1, k2tog. (3 sts)

Row 18: Sl 1, p2tog, psso. (1 st)

Fasten off, weave in ends, and block flat.

Berries

Make 22

With smaller needles and B, cast on 3 sts, leaving a 12-inch tail.

Row 1: Inc, k1, inc. (5 sts)

Rows 2, 4, 6: Purl.

Row 3: Inc, k3, inc. (7 sts)

Row 5 and 7: Knit.

Row 8: [P2tog] 3 times, k1. (4 sts)

Row 9: [K2tog] twice. (2 sts)

Bind off.

Turn berries inside out so that the purl side is showing. Use the cast-on tail and tapestry needle to sew and gather sides tog into a ball shape. Fasten off, weave in ends.

Finishing

Block throw to finished measurements to open up the lace sts.

Arrange holly leaves and berries along top and bottom borders of throw (see photographs). Pin in place. Using the sewing thread and needle, tack holly in place using an invisible st. ❊

Cozy Throw for Grandpa

Grandpa will love this afghan, no matter which side is up—it's reversible!

 EASY

Design by Kristin Omdahl

Finished Size

Approx 45 x 55 inches

Materials

- Plymouth Yukon Print 35 percent mohair/35 percent wool/30 percent acrylic super bulky weight yarn (59 yds/100g per ball): 12 balls green/gray multi #8004
- Size 15 (10mm) 29-inch circular needle or size needed to obtain gauge
- Tapestry needle

Gauge

9 sts and 14 rows = 5 inches/12.5cm in lace st

To save time, take time to check gauge.

Pattern Stitches

A. Seed St (odd number of sts)

Row 1: K1, *p1, k1; rep from * to end. Rep Row 1 for pat.

B. Lace Pat A (multiple of 50 sts)

Row 1 (RS): [K6, k2tog, yo] 3 times, k2, [yo, ssk, k6] 3 times.

Row 2: [P7, k1] 3 times, p2, [k1, p7] 3 times.

Row 3: [K5, k2tog, yo, p1] 3 times, k2, [p1, yo, ssk, k5] 3 times.

Row 4: [P6, k2] 3 times, p2, [k2, p6] 3 times.

Row 5: [K4, k2tog, yo, p2] 3 times, k2, [p2, yo, ssk, k4] 3 times.

Row 6: [P5, k3] 3 times, p2, [k3, p5] 3 times.

Row 7: [K3, k2tog, yo, p3] 3 times, k2, [p3, yo, ssk, k3] 3 times.

Row 8: [P4, k4] 3 times, p2, [k4, p4] 3 times.

Row 9: [K2, k2tog, yo, p4] 3 times, k2, [p4, yo, ssk, k2] 3 times.

Row 10: [P3, k5] 3 times, p2, [k5, p3] 3 times.

Row 11: [K1, k2tog, yo, p5] 3 times, k2, [p5, yo, ssk, k1] 3 times.

Row 12: [P2, k6] 3 times, p2, [k6, p2] 3 times.

Row 13: [K2tog, yo, p6] 3 times, k2, [p6, yo, ssk] 3 times.

Row 14: [P1, k7] 3 times, p2, [k7, p1] 3 times.

Rep Rows 1–14 for pat.

C. Lace Pat B (multiple of 50 sts)

Row 1 (RS): K1, [yo, ssk, k6] 3 times, [k6, k2tog, yo] 3 times, k1.

Row 2: P1, [k1, p7] 3 times, [p7, k1] 3 times, p1.

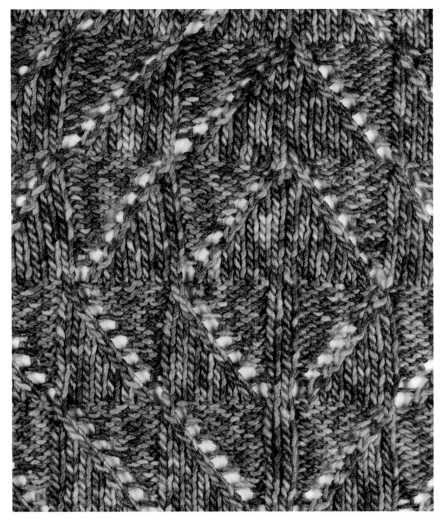

Row 11: K1 [p5, yo, ssk, k1] 3 times, [k1, k2tog, yo, p5] 3 times, k1.

Row 12: P1, [k6, p2] 3 times, [p2, k5] 3 times, p1.

Row 13: K1, [p6, yo, ssk] 3 times, [k2tog, yo, p6] 3 times, k1.

Row 14: P1, [k7, p1] 3 times, [p1, k7] 3 times, p1.

Rep Rows 1–14 for pat.

Pattern Notes

The afghan is worked back and forth in rows; a circular needle is used to accommodate the large number of sts.

Charts for the Lace patterns are included for those preferring to work from charts. Chart A is for Lace Pat A and Chart B is for Lace Pat B.

Afghan

Cast on 105 sts.

Work in Seed St for 3 rows.

Next row: Continue in Seed St and inc 1 st in middle of row. (106 sts)

Next row (RS): Work 3 sts in Seed St, work 2 reps of Lace Pat A across next 100 sts, work 3 sts in Seed St.

Maintaining first and last 3 sts in Seed St, complete 3 reps of Lace Pat A as established, 3 reps of Lace Pat B, and 3 reps of Lace Pat A.

Next row: Work in Seed St and dec 1 st in middle of row. (105 sts)

Continue in Seed St as established for 3 rows.

Bind off loosely.

Weave in loose ends.

Wash, block and dry to finished measurements. ✳

Row 3: K1, [p1, yo, ssk, k5] 3 times, [k5, k2tog, yo, p1] 3 times, k1.

Row 4: P1, [k2, p6] 3 times, [p6, k2] 3 times, p1.

Row 5: K1, [p2, yo, ssk, k4] 3 times, [k4, k2tog, yo, p2] 3 times, k1.

Row 6: P1, [k3, p5] 3 times, [p5, k3] 3 times, p1.

Row 7: K1, [p3, yo, ssk, k3] 3 times, [k3, k2tog, yo, p3] 3 times, k1.

Row 8: P1, [k4, p4] 3 times, [p4, k4] 3 times, p1.

Row 9: K1, [p4, yo, ssk, k2] 3 times, [k2, k2tog, yo, p4] 3 times, k1.

Row 10: P1, [k5, p3] 3 times, [p3, k5] 3 times, p1.

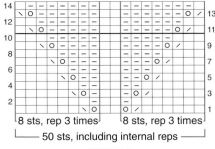

8 sts, rep 3 times | 8 sts, rep 3 times
50 sts, including internal reps

CHART A

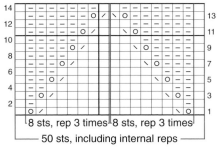

8 sts, rep 3 times | 8 sts, rep 3 times
50 sts, including internal reps

CHART B

STITCH KEY
- ☐ K on RS, p on WS
- − P on RS, k on WS
- ╱ K2tog
- ╲ Ssk
- ○ Yo

Glamour Throw for Grandma

Self-striping yarns make this stunning throw super-easy to knit—it's even self-fringing!

 EASY

Design by Julie Gaddy

Finished Size

Approx 45 x 55 inches (excluding fringe)

Materials

- Plymouth Tomorrow 40 percent nylon/38 percent mohair/18 percent acrylic/4 percent metal bulky weight yarn (82 yds/50g per ball): 5 balls lilac/light orange/pale yellow multi #1607 (A) **[5 BULKY]**
- Plymouth Yesterday 80 percent mohair/15 percent wool/5 percent nylon bulky weight yarn (110 yds/50g per ball): 4 balls lilac/light orange/pale yellow multi #1607 (B)
- Plymouth Today 80 percent mohair/15 percent wool/5 percent nylon bulky weight yarn (100 yds/50g per ball): 5 balls lilac/light orange/pale yellow multi #1607 (C)
- Size 17 (12mm) circular needle or size needed to obtain gauge

Gauge

6 sts and 10 rows = 4 inches/10cm in Seed St

To save time, take time to check gauge.

Pattern Stitch

Seed St (odd number of sts)
Row 1: K1, *p1, k1; rep from * to end.
Rep Row 1 for pat.

Pattern Notes

This throw is worked back and forth in rows from side-to-side; a circular needle is used to accommodate the large number of sts.

The throw is worked holding 2 strands of yarn tog throughout; the yarns change on every row according to the sequence in the pat below.

For fringes, leave 9-inch tails when attaching and cutting yarns.

Throw

With A and B held tog and leaving a 9-inch tail, loosely cast on 75 sts.

Cut yarns leaving a 9-inch tail, turn.

With B and C held tog, leaving a 9-inch tail at beg of row, work 1 row in Seed St. Cut yarns, leaving a 9-inch tail.

Using an overhand knot, tie tails at beg of row (AB from cast on and BC), forming fringe.

With C and A held tog, *leaving a 9-inch tail at beg of row, work 1 row Seed St. Cut yarns, leaving a 9-inch tail. Using an overhand knot, tie tails (BC and CA) at beg of row as before.*

Rep from * to *, changing yarns on every row in AB-BC-CA sequence, until throw measures approx 45 inches (for width) from beg.

Bind off loosely.

Lay throw on a large flat surface and trim ends of fringe even.

Block lightly. ❋

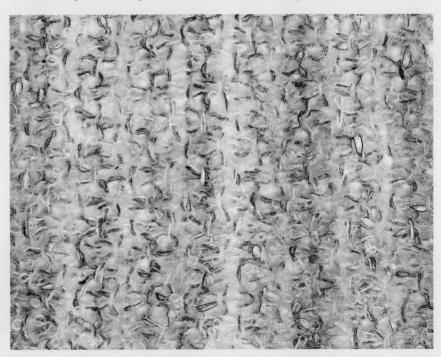

Quick Festive Throw

This warm and thick throw (or afghan) knits up quickly in an easily memorized pattern using two different needle sizes to add texture.

Design by Gaye Walker

Sizes
Throw (afghan) Instructions are given for smaller size, with larger size in parentheses. When only 1 number is given, it applies to both sizes.

Finished Measurements
Approx 35 x 40 (48 x 55) inches (excluding fringe)

Materials
- Plymouth Hand Paint Wool 100 percent wool super bulky weight yarn (60 yds/100g per skein): 13 (20) skeins orange-pink #170 **6 SUPER BULKY**
- Size 10 (6mm) 29-inch circular needle or size needed to obtain gauge
- Size 17 (12.75mm) 29-inch circular needle or size needed to obtain gauge
- Size H/8 (5mm) crochet hook
- Tapestry needle

Gauge
10 sts and 13 rows = 4 inches/10cm in pat st with larger and smaller needles
To save time, take time to check gauge.

Pattern Stitch
(even number of sts)
Row 1 (RS): With smaller needle, *k1-tbl, p1; rep from * to end.
Row 2: With larger needle, * k1, p1; rep from * to end.
Rep Rows 1 and 2 for pat.

Pattern Notes
The throw is worked back and forth in rows; circular needles are used to accommodate the large number of sts.

If it is necessary to change needle sizes to obtain gauge, the larger needle should be 5 U.S. sizes larger than the smaller needle.

The fringe uses approximately 3 (5) hanks.

Throw (Afghan)
With smaller needle, cast on 88 (136) sts.

Beg with Row 1, work in pat until piece measures 40 (55) inches from beg, ending with a WS row.

Bind off on RS in pat.

Weave in all ends.

Triple-Knot Fringe
Cut 264 (408) 25-inch strands yarn.

*Fold 1 group of 3 strands in half. With RS facing and beg at corner of 1 edge, use crochet hook to draw folded end from RS to WS. Pull loose ends through folded section. Draw knot up firmly. Rep from *, attaching 1 (3-strand) fringe in every other st across bottom of throw (afghan).

*Divide strands, using 3 from left and 3 from right groups, and tie in square knot approx 1½ inches below first row of knots. Rep from * across each end.

Rep for another row of knots.

Rep fringe along top of throw.

Trim even. ❄

Garter Stitch Gift Afghan

Worked in separate garter-stitch squares, this afghan is the perfect carry-along project!

 BEGINNER

Design by Cindy Adams

Finished Size
Approx 45 x 63 inches

Materials
- Plymouth Encore Worsted 75 percent acrylic/25 percent wool medium weight yarn (200 yds/100g per ball): 5 balls green #1232 (A), 4 balls red #9601 (B) and 2 balls natural #146 (C)
- Size 7 (4.5mm) straight needles or size needed to obtain gauge
- Size H/8 (5mm) crochet hook
- Tapestry needle
- White sewing thread
- Sewing needle

Gauge
14 sts and 28 rows = 4 inches/10cm in garter st
To save time, take time to check gauge.

Pattern Note
On all rows, sl the first st with yarn in front.

Afghan

Green Blocks
Make 17
With A, cast on 30 sts.
Knit 60 rows.
Bind off.
Weave in all ends.

Package Blocks
Make 18
With B, cast on 30 sts.
Knit 24 rows.
Cut B and attach C.

Knit 12 rows.
Cut C and attach B.
Knit 24 rows.
Bind off.
Weave in all ends.

I-Cord Bows
Make 18
With C, cast on 4 sts.
*K4, do not turn, sl sts back to LH needle; rep from * until cord measures 20 inches. Bind off.
Weave in all ends.
Tie into bow.

Assembly
Arrange blocks referring to photo, alternating Green and Package Blocks.
Note: Garter st on Green Blocks runs horizontally; garter st on Package Blocks runs vertically.
With RS tog, using crochet hook and A, sl st blocks tog.
With sewing thread and needle, tack bow-knot to center top of C area of Package Block, then tack each bow-loop and hanging end. ✳

A Knitter's Tree Throw

Knit one piece at a time and sewn like a quilt, this Christmas tree can be embellished as you wish.

 EASY

Design by Sara Louise Harper

Sizes
Crib (lap, blanket) Instructions are given for smallest size, with larger sizes in parentheses. When only 1 number is given, it applies to all sizes.

Finished Measurements
Approx 24 x 36 (48 x 60, 64 x 78) inches

Materials
- Plymouth Merino Supreme 100 percent merino wool medium weight yarn (65 yds/50g per ball): 4 (12, 21) balls green #2222 (A); 6 (18, 32) balls cream #2200 (B); 1 ball brown #2224 (C); 2 (5, 8) balls red #2209 (D)
- Size 9 (5.5mm) straight and 29-inch (36-inch, 36-inch) circular needle, or size needed to obtain gauge
- Tapestry needle
- Sewing needle and thread
- Assorted buttons

Gauge
16 sts and 30 rows = 4 inches/10cm in garter st.
To save time, take time to check gauge.

Special Abbreviation
Inc (Increase): Inc 1 by knitting in front and back of st.

Cream Squares
Make 4
With B, cast on 20 (32, 44) sts.
Work in garter st until piece measures 5 (8, 11) inches.
Bind off.

Green Squares
Make 6
With A, cast on 20 (32, 44) sts.
Work in garter st until piece measures 5 (8, 11) inches.
Bind off.

Cream Half-Squares
Make 4
With B, cast on 10 (16, 22) sts.
Work in garter st until piece measures 5 (8, 11) inches.
Bind off.

Diagonally Knit Squares
Make 8
With B, cast on 2 sts.
Inc row: Inc in first st, knit to end of row.
Rep Inc row until there are 32 (44, 56) sts on needle.
Cut B and attach A.
Knit 1 row.
Dec row: Ssk, knit to end of row.
Rep Dec row until 1 st remains.
Cut yarn and fasten off.

Large Cream Rectangles
Make 2
With B, cast on 46 (76, 106) sts.
Work in garter st until piece measures 10 (16, 22) inches.
Bind off.

Tree Trunk
With C, cast on 36 (60, 84) sts.
Work in garter st until piece measures 2 inches.
Bind off.

Finishing
Lay out all pieces following assembly diagram.
Sew pieces tog in rows, then sew rows tog to form body of afghan.
Block afghan gently.

ASSEMBLY DIAGRAM

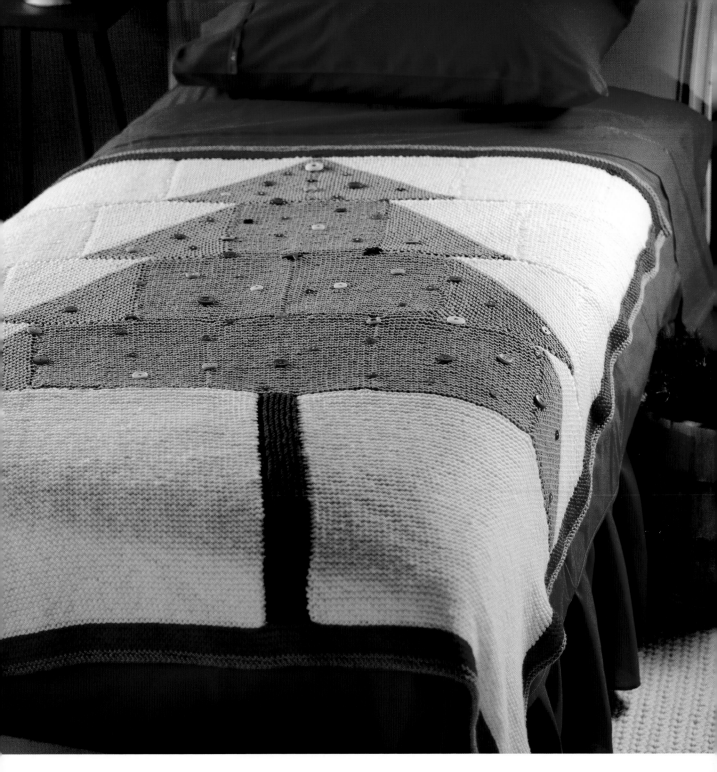

First Border

With RS facing, circular needle and D, pick up and knit approx 140 (190, 300) sts along 1 side of afghan.

Work in garter st for 10 rows, then bind off loosely.

Rep on other side.

Pick up and knit approx 125 (180, 250) sts along the bottom edge of afghan.

Work in garter st for 10 rows, then bind off loosely.

Rep on top.

Second Border

With RS facing, circular needle and A, work borders separately as for First Border, picking up and knitting approx 156 (206, 316) sts along sides and approx 140 (196, 266) sts along top and bottom of afghan.

Work each edge's border in garter st for 4 rows, then bind off sts loosely.

Weave in all ends, and block again if necessary.

With sewing needle and thread, embellish tree (green area) with buttons as desired. ❄

Glorious Gift Throw

This warm, light-as-air throw is knitted in a simple slip-stitch pattern, alternating two rows of variegated mohair blend with two rows of worsted weight wool, and finished with a generous fringe.

 EASY

Design by Sara Louise Harper

Sizes
Throw (afghan) Instructions are given for smaller size, with larger size in parentheses. When only 1 number is given, it applies to both sizes.

Finished Measurements
Approx 35 x 40 (48 x 55) inches (excluding fringe)

Materials
- Plymouth Yesterday 80 percent mohair/15 percent wool/5 percent nylon bulky weight yarn (110 yds/50g per ball): 8 (13) balls orange-variegated #1663 (A)
- Plymouth Galway Worsted 100 percent wool medium weight yarn (210 yds/100g per ball): 3 (5) balls mauve #19 (B)
- Size 11 (8mm) 29-inch circular needle or size needed to obtain gauge
- Size H/8 (5mm) crochet hook
- Tapestry needle

Gauge
15 sts and 23 rows = 4 inches/10cm in pattern st
To save time, take time to check gauge.

Pattern Stitch
(odd number of sts)
Row 1 (WS): With A, purl.
Row 2: With B, k1, *sl 1 knitwise, k1; rep from * across.
Row 3: With B, k1, *sl 1 purlwise, k1; rep from * across.
Row 4: With A, knit.
Rep Rows 1–4 for pat.

Pattern Notes
The throw is worked back and forth in rows; a circular needle is used to accommodate the large number of sts.

Do not cut yarn when changing colors; twist yarns and carry yarn not in use up side.

Fringe uses approximately 2 (4) skeins of A.

Throw (Afghan)
With A, cast on 131 (181) sts.
Work in pat until piece measures 40 (55) inches from beg, ending with Row 4.
With A, bind off purlwise.
Weave in all ends.

Finishing
Rnd 1: With RS facing, beg at bottom right corner, using crochet hook and A, work 1 rnd of sc evenly around all 4 edges, working 3 sc in each corner; join in top of first sc. Do not cut yarn.
Rnd 2: With RS facing, *[sc, ch 3, skip 2, sc] across bottom to corner; work 2 sc in corner; sc in each sc to corner; work 2 sc in corner; rep from * along top and other side; join in top of first sc.
Cut yarn.
Weave in all ends.

Fringe
Cut 6 (16-inch) strands of A for fringe in each crochet lp on top and bottom of throw. *Fold 1 group of 6 strands in half. With RS facing and beg at corner of 1 edge, use crochet hook to draw folded end from RS to WS. Pull loose ends through folded section. Draw knot up firmly. Rep from *, attaching 1 (6-strand) fringe in each of the crochet lps. Trim even. ❈

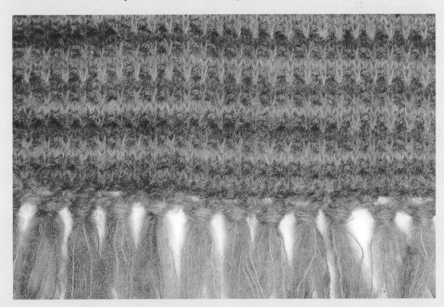

Plaid-to-Meet-You Throw

Inspired by plaid, this is an afghan to bring out for the holidays—then leave it out all year!

Design by Sara Louise Harper

Sizes
Crib (lap, blanket) Instructions are given for smallest size, with larger sizes in parentheses. When only 1 number is given, it applies to all sizes.

Finished Measurements
24 x 36 (48 x 60, 64 x 78) inches (excluding fringe)

Materials
- Plymouth Encore Chunky 75 percent acrylic/25 percent wool bulky weight yarn (143 yds/100g per ball): 4 (11, 19) balls green #3335 (A); 1 (1, 2) balls each red #174 (B) and pink #137 (C)
- Size 10 (6mm) 32-inch (32-inch, 36-inch) circular needle or size needed to obtain gauge
- Tapestry needle
- Crochet hook (for attaching fringe)

Gauge
14 sts and 18 rows = 4 inches/10cm in St st
To save time, take time to check gauge.

Pattern Notes
Throw is worked back and forth in rows; a circular needle is used to accommodate the large number of sts.

Use separate lengths for colors B and C, stranding A behind on WS.

Throw
With A, cast on 84 (168, 224) sts.

Set-up row: K16 (32, 42) A; k2 B; k16 (18, 20) A; k2 C; k30 (70, 100) A; k2 B; k16 (42, 56) A.

Knit next 4 rows in colors as established.

Keeping first and last 2 sts in garter st throughout, work 32 (58, 82) rows in St st in pat at established.

Next row (RS): Attach C and knit to first vertical B stripe, k2 B, knit with C to end.

Next row: With C, purl to 2nd vertical B stripe, p2 B, purl with C to end. Cut C.

Work original color pat in St st for 30 (27, 78) rows.

Next row (RS): Attach B and knit to vertical C stripe, k2 C, knit with B to end.

Next row: With B, purl to vertical C stripe, p2 C, purl with B to end. Cut B.

Work original color pat in St st for 50 (110, 100) rows.

Next row (RS): Attach C and knit to 2nd vertical B stripe, k2 B, knit with C to end.

Next row: With C, purl to first vertical B stripe, p2 B, purl with C to end. Cut C.

Work original color pat in St st for 36 (50, 76) rows.

Knit 4 rows in color pat.
Bind off.
Weave in all ends.
Block.

Fringe
Cut 20-inch lengths of yarn for fringe. *Fold 1 or 2 strands (as desired) in half. With RS facing and beg at corner of 1 short edge, use crochet hook to draw folded end from RS to WS. Pull loose ends through folded section. Draw knot up firmly. Rep from * across, spacing fringes approx every 3 sts and matching fringes to vertical stripe colors. Trim even. ❈

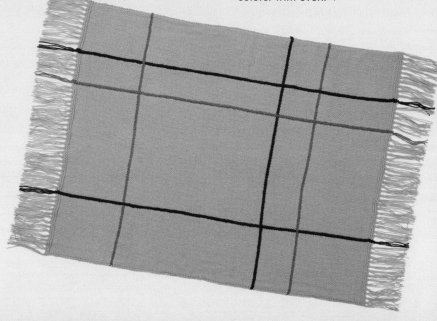

Tipsy Cables Throw

Openwork cables tilt at slight angles as they meander along the length of this casual throw.

 INTERMEDIATE

Design by Diane Zangl

Finished Size
Approx 45 x 55 inches

Materials
- Plymouth Merino Supreme 100 percent merino wool medium weight yarn (65 yds/50g per ball): 31 balls red #2209
- Size 9 (5.5mm) 36-inch circular needle or size needed to obtain gauge
- Cable needle
- Stitch markers
- Tapestry needle

Gauge
17 sts and 21 rows = 4 inches/10cm in Tipsy Cable pat

To save time, take time to check gauge.

Pattern Stitch
Tipsy Cables (multiple of 14 sts + 9)
See Chart.

Pattern Notes
Afghan is worked back and forth in rows; circular needle is used to accommodate the large number of sts.

Sl first st of every row.

Throw
Cast on 173 sts.

Slipping first st of every row, knit 7 rows.

Set-up row (RS): Sl 1, k4, place marker, work Row 1 of chart to last 5 sts, place marker, k5.

Slipping first st of every row and maintaining 5 sts at each edge in garter st and remainder in pat from chart, work even until throw measures approx 54 inches from beg, ending with Row 1 of pat.

Slipping first st of every row, knit 7 rows.

Bind off knitwise.

Weave in all ends.

Block as necessary. ❋

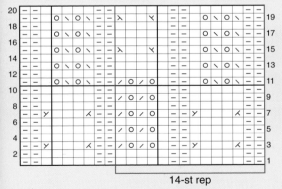

TIPSY CABLES THROW

14-st rep

STITCH KEY
- ☐ K on RS, p on WS
- ⊟ P on RS, k on WS
- ⊡ Yo
- ⊿ K2tog
- ⊠ Ssk
- ⟋‾‾‾‾⟍ Sl 3 to cn and hold in front, k2, k3, from cn
- ⟍‾‾‾‾⟋ Sl 2 to cn and hold in back, k3, k2 from cn

Babes in Dreamland Blanket

This afghan will surely become a favorite—it combines an easy pattern with a scrumptious yarn.

◀■□◻ EASY

Design by Sara Louise Harper

Sizes

Crib (lap, blanket) Instructions are given for smallest size, with larger sizes in parentheses. When only 1 number is given, it applies to all sizes.

Finished Measurements

Approx 24 x 40 (48 x 60, 64 x 78) inches

Materials

- Plymouth Oh My! 100 percent nylon bulky weight yarn (70 yds/50g per ball): 4 (12, 21) balls green #19 (A), 4 (12, 21) balls pale yellow #12 (B) and 4 (12, 21) balls red #23 (C)

  5 BULKY

- Size 10½ (6.5mm) 24-inch (29-inch, 36-inch) circular needle or size needed to obtain gauge
- Tapestry needle

Gauge

15 sts and 24 rows = 4 inches/10cm in St st
To save time, take time to check gauge.

Pattern Notes

The blanket is worked back and forth in rows; a circular needle is used to accommodate the large number of sts.

Cut yarn after each stripe, leaving a tail to weave in.

Work first and last 3 sts in garter st for edge.

Blanket

With B, cast on 90 (180, 240) sts.

Knit 6 rows.

Maintaining first and last 3 sts in garter st throughout, work St st stripes as follows:

62 (104, 134) rows B.

6 (10, 14) rows C.

2 (6, 8) rows B.

2 (6, 8) rows A.

58 (100, 130) rows C.

2 (6, 8) rows B.

2 (6, 8) rows A.

6 (10, 14) rows C.

62 (104, 134) rows A.

With A, knit 6 rows.

Bind off.

Weave in all ends.

No blocking should be necessary. ❋

Santa's Baby Blankie

From cuddly infants to huggable toddlers, kiddies of all ages will enjoy this soft blankie

◼◼◻◻ EASY

Design by Anita Closic

Finished Size
Approx 28 x 36 inches

Materials
- Plymouth Heaven 100 percent nylon super bulky weight yarn (55 yds/50g per ball): 2 balls white #9 (A) **[6 SUPER BULKY]**
- Plymouth Oh My! 100 percent nylon bulky weight yarn (70 yds/50g per ball): 6 balls red #23 (B) **[5 BULKY]**
- Size 10 (6mm) 29-inch circular needle
- Size 11 (8mm) 29-inch circular needle or size needed to obtain gauge
- Tapestry needle

Gauge
12 sts and 13 rows = 4 inches/10cm in Lace pat with larger needles
To save time, take time to check gauge.

Pattern Stitch
Lace (multiple of 10 sts + 15)
Row 1 (RS): K2, k2tog, *k3, yo, k1, yo, k3, sl 1, k2tog, psso; rep from * to last 11 sts, k3, yo, k1, yo, k3, k2tog, k2.
Row 2: K2, purl to last 2 sts, k2.
Rep Rows 1 and 2 for pat.

Pattern Notes
Use smaller needle when knitting with A and larger needle when knitting with B.

The blanket is worked back and forth in rows; circular needles are used to accommodate the large number of sts.

Carry B up side of work when not in use, twisting around A at beg of row.

Blanket
With smaller needle and A, cast on 85 sts.
Knit 2 rows.

*Change to larger needle and B, and work 10 rows of Lace pat.
Change to smaller needle and A, and knit 2 rows.
Rep from * 9 times.
Bind off loosely.
Weave in all ends. ❄

Knitting Stitch Guide

CAST ON

Leaving an end about an inch long for each stitch to be cast on, make a slip knot on the right needle.

Place the thumb and index finger of your left hand between the yarn ends with the long yarn end over your thumb, and the strand from the skein over your index finger. Close your other fingers over the strands to hold them against your palm. Spread your thumb and index fingers apart and draw the yarn into a "V."

Place the needle in front of the strand around your thumb and bring it underneath this strand. Carry the needle over and under the strand on your index finger.

Draw through loop on thumb.

Drop the loop from your thumb and draw up the strand to form a stitch on the needle.

Repeat until you have cast on the number of stitches indicated in the pattern. Remember to count the beginning slip knot as a stitch.

CABLE CAST ON

This type of cast on is used when adding stitches in the middle or at the end of a row. Make a slip knot on the left needle.

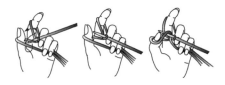

Knit a stitch in this knot and place it on the left needle.

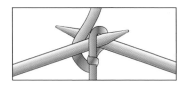

Insert the right needle between the last two stitches on the left needle. Knit a stitch and place it on the left needle. Repeat for each stitch needed.

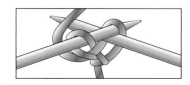

KNIT (K)

Insert tip of right needle from front to back in next stitch on left needle.

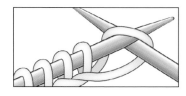

Bring yarn under and over the tip of the right needle.

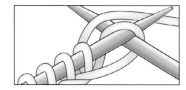

Pull yarn loop through the stitch with right needle point.

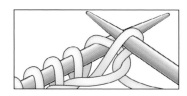

Slide the stitch off the left needle. The new stitch is on the right needle.

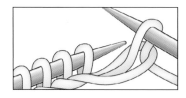

PURL (P)

With yarn in front, insert tip of right needle from back to front through next stitch on the left needle.

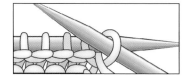

Bring yarn around the right needle counterclockwise.

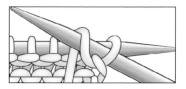

With right needle, draw yarn back through the stitch.

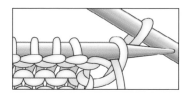

Slide the stitch off the left needle. The new stitch is on the right needle.

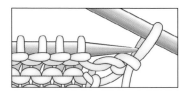

BIND OFF

Binding off (knit)

Knit first two stitches on left needle. Insert tip of left needle into first stitch worked on right needle and pull it over the second stitch and completely off the needle.

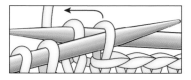

Knit the next stitch and repeat. When one stitch remains on right needle, cut yarn and draw tail through last stitch to fasten off.

Binding off (purl)

Purl first two stitches on left needle. Insert tip of left needle into first stitch worked on right needle and pull it over the second stitch and completely off the needle.

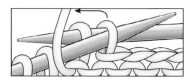

Purl the next stitch and repeat. When one stitch remains on right needle, cut yarn and draw tail through last stitch to fasten off.

INCREASE (INC)

Two-stitches-in-one-stitch increase (knit)

Knit the next stitch in the usual manner, but don't remove the stitch from the left needle. Place right needle behind left needle and knit again into the back of the same stitch. Slip original stitch off left needle.

Two-stitches-in-one-stitch increase (purl)

Purl the next stitch in the usual manner, but don't remove the stitch from the left needle. Place right needle behind left needle and purl again into the back of the same stitch. Slip original stitch off left needle.

INVISIBLE INCREASE (M1)

There are several ways to make or increase one stitch.

Make 1 with Left Twist (M1L)

Insert left needle from front to back under the horizontal strand between the last stitch worked and next stitch on left needle.

With right needle, knit into the back of this loop.

To make this increase on the purl side, insert left needle in same manner and purl into the back of the loop.

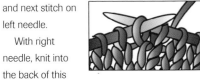

Make 1 with Right Twist (M1R)

Insert left needle from back to front under the horizontal strand between the last stitch worked and next stitch on left needle.

With right needle, knit into the front of this loop.

To make this increase on the purl side, insert left needle in same manner and purl into the front of the loop.

Make 1 with Backward Loop over the right needle

With your thumb, make a loop over the right needle.

Slip the loop from your thumb onto the needle and pull to tighten.

Make 1 in top of stitch below

Insert tip of right needle into the stitch on left needle one row below.

Knit this stitch; then knit the stitch on the left needle.

DECREASE (DEC)

Knit 2 together (k2tog)

Put tip of right needle through next two stitches on left needle as to knit. Knit these two stitches as one.

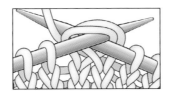

Purl 2 together (p2tog)

Put tip of right needle through next two stitches on left needle as to purl. Purl these two stitches as one.

Slip, Slip, Knit (ssk)

Slip next two stitches, one at a time, as to knit from left needle to right needle.

Insert left needle in front of both stitches and work off needle together.

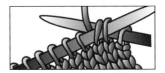

Slip, Slip, Purl (ssp)

Slip next two stitches, one at a time, as to knit from left needle to right needle. Slip these stitches back onto left needle keeping them twisted.

Purl these two stitches together through back loops.

General Information

Felting Instructions

Place items to be felted in the washing machine along with one tablespoon of dish soap and a pair of jeans or other laundry. (Remember, do not wash felting with other clothing that releases its own fibers, or you will have these fibers in your project.) Set washing machine on smallest load using hot water. Start the machine and check the progress after ten minutes. Check progress more frequently after piece starts to felt. Reset the machine, if needed, to continue the agitation cycle. Do not allow machine to drain and spin until the piece is the desired size; creases can form in the fabric during the rapid spin cycle. As the piece becomes more felted, you may need to pull it into shape. When the piece has felted to the desired size, rinse it by hand in warm water—a cold-water rinse will continue the felting process. Remove the excess water either by rolling in a towel and squeezing, or in the spin cycle of your washing machine.

Block the piece into shape, and let air dry. Do not dry in clothes dryer. Felted items are very strong, so don't be afraid to push and pull it into the desired shape. It may take several hours or several days for the pieces to dry completely.

After the piece is completely dry, excess fuzziness can be trimmed with scissors if a smoother surface is desired. Or the piece can be brushed for a fuzzier appearance.

A Word About Gauge

A correct stitch gauge is very important. Please take the time to work a stitch gauge swatch about 4 x 4 inches. Measure the swatch. If the number of stitches and rows are fewer than indicated under "Gauge" in the pattern, your needles are too large. Try another swatch with smaller needles. If the number of stitches and rows are more than indicated under "Gauge" in the pattern, your needles are too small. Try another swatch with larger needles.

Crochet Chain Stitch

Chain—ch: Yo, pull through lp on hook.

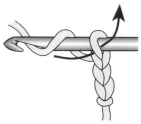

3-Needle Bind Off

Use this technique for seaming two edges together, such as when joining a shoulder seam. Hold the edge stitches on two separate needles with right sides together.

With a third needle, knit together a stitch from the front needle with one from the back.

Repeat, knitting a stitch from the front needle with one from the back needle once more.

Slip the first stitch over the second.

Repeat knitting, a front and back pair of stitches together, then bind one off.

Fringe

Cut a piece of cardboard half as long as specified in instructions for strands plus ½ inch for trimming. Wind yarn loosely and evenly around cardboard. When cardboard is filled, cut yarn across one end. Do this several times; then begin fringing. Wind additional strands as necessary.

Single Knot Fringe

Cut a piece of cardboard half as long as specified in instructions for strands plus ½ inch for trimming. Wind yarn loosely and evenly around cardboard. When cardboard is filled, cut yarn across one end. Do this several times; then begin fringing. Wind additional strands as necessary.

Hold specified number of strands for one knot together; fold in half. Hold project to be fringed with right side facing you. Use crochet hook to draw folded end through space or stitch indicated from right to wrong side.

Pull loose ends through folded section. Draw knot up firmly. Space knots as indicated in pattern instructions.

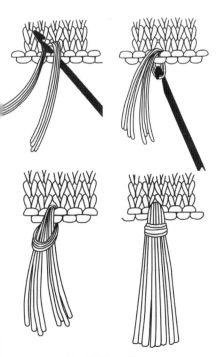

Single Knot Fringe

Double Knot Fringe

Begin by working Single Knot Fringe completely across one end of piece. With right side facing you and working from left to right, take half the strands of one knot and half the strands of the knot next to it and knot them together.

Double Knot Fringe

Triple Knot Fringe

Begin by working Single Knot Fringe completely across one end of piece. With right side facing you and working from left to right, take half the strands of one knot and half the strands of the knot next to it and knot them together. Continuing on the right side, work from left to right tying a third row of knots.

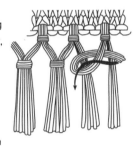

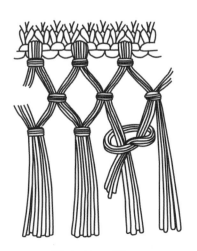

Triple Knot Fringe

Kitchener Stitch

This method of grafting two sets of live stitches is used for the toes of socks and flat seams. To weave the edges together and form an unbroken line of stockinette stitch, divide all stitches evenly onto two knitting needles—one behind the other. Thread yarn into tapestry needle. Hold needles with wrong sides together and work from right to left as follows:

Step 1: Insert tapestry needle into first stitch on front needle as to purl. Draw yarn through stitch, leaving stitch on knitting needle.

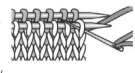

Step 2: Insert tapestry needle into the first stitch on the back needle as to purl. Draw yarn through stitch and slip stitch off knitting needle.

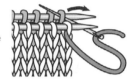

Step 3: Insert tapestry needle into the next stitch on same (back) needle as to knit, leaving stitch on knitting needle.

Step 4: Insert tapestry needle into the first stitch on the front needle as to knit. Draw yarn through stitch and slip stitch off knitting needle.

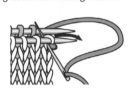

Step 5: Insert tapestry needle into the next stitch on same (front) needle as to purl. Draw yarn through stitch, leaving stitch on knitting needle.

Repeat Steps 2 through 5 until one stitch is left on each needle. Then repeat Steps 2 and 4. Fasten off. Woven stitches should be the same size as adjacent knitted stitches.

General Information

Standard Abbreviations

[ ] work instructions within brackets as many times as directed

( ) work instructions within parentheses in the place directed

** repeat instructions following the asterisks as directed

* repeat instructions following the single asterisk as directed

" inch(es)

approx approximately

beg begin/beginning

CC contrasting color

ch chain stitch

cm centimeter(s)

cn cable needle

dec decrease/decreases/ decreasing

dpn(s) double-pointed needle(s)

g gram

inc increase/increases/ increasing

k knit

k2tog knit 2 stitches together

LH left hand

lp(s) loop(s)

m meter(s)

M1 make one stitch

MC main color

mm millimeter(s)

oz ounce(s)

p purl

pat(s) pattern(s)

p2tog purl 2 stitches together

psso pass slipped stitch over

psso2 pass 2 slipped stitches over

rem remain/remaining

rep repeat(s)

rev St st reverse Stockinette stitch

RH right hand

rnd(s) rounds

RS right side

skp slip, knit, pass stitch over—one stitch decreased

sk2p slip 1, knit 2 together, pass slip stitch over the knit 2 together— two stitches decreased

sl slip

sl 1k slip 1 knitwise

sl 1p slip 1 purlwise

sl st slip stitch(es)

ssk slip, slip, knit these 2 stitches together— a decrease

ssp slip next 2 stitches as to knit, slip back to left needle and purl together through back loops— a decrease

st(s) stitch(es)

St st stockinette stitch/ stocking stitch

tbl through back loop(s)

tog together

WS wrong side

wyib with yarn in back

wyif with yarn in front

yd(s) yard(s)

yfwd yarn forward

yo yarn over

Skill Levels

BEGINNER

Projects for first-time knitters using basic knit and purl stitches. Minimal shaping.

EASY

Projects using basic stitches, repetitive stitch patterns, simple color changes and simple shaping and finishing.

INTERMEDIATE

Projects with a variety of stitches, such as basic cables and lace, simple intarsia, double-pointed needles and knitting in the round needle techniques, mid-level shaping and finishing.

EXPERIENCED

Projects using advanced techniques and stitches, such as short rows, Fair Isle, more intricate intarsia, cables, lace patterns and numerous color changes.

Glossary

bind off—used to finish an edge

cast on—process of making foundation stitches used in knitting

decrease—means of reducing the number of stitches in a row

increase—means of adding to the number of stitches in a row

intarsia—method of knitting a multicolored pattern into the fabric

knitwise—insert needle into stitch as if to knit

make 1—method of increasing using the strand between the last stitch worked and the next stitch

place marker—placing a purchased marker or loop of contrasting yarn onto the needle for ease in working a pattern repeat or into the fabric to mark a given position

purlwise—insert needle into stitch as if to purl

right side—side of garment or piece that will be seen when worn

selvage stitch—edge stitch used to make seaming easier

slip, slip, knit—a left-leaning decrease which mirrors the right-leaning "knit 2 together" decrease

slip stitch—an unworked stitch slipped from left needle to right needle, usually as if to purl

wrong side—side that will be inside when garment is worn

work even—continue to work in the pattern as established without working any increases or decreases

work in pattern as established— continue to work following the pattern stitch as it has been set up or established on the needle, working any increases or decreases in such a way that the established pattern remains the same

yarn over—method of increasing by wrapping the yarn over the right needle without working a stitch

General Information

INCHES INTO MILLIMETERS & CENTIMETERS (Rounded off slightly)

inches	mm	cm	inches	cm	inches	cm	inches	cm
1/8	3	0.3	5	12.5	21	53.5	38	96.5
1/4	6	0.6	5 1/2	14	22	56	39	99
3/8	10	1	6	15	23	58.5	40	101.5
1/2	13	1.3	7	18	24	61	41	104
5/8	15	1.5	8	20.5	25	63.5	42	106.5
3/4	20	2	9	23	26	66	43	109
7/8	22	2.2	10	25.5	27	68.5	44	112
1	25	2.5	11	28	28	71	45	114.5
1 1/4	32	3.2	12	30.5	29	73.5	46	117
1 1/2	38	3.8	13	33	30	76	47	119.5
1 3/4	45	4.5	14	35.5	31	79	48	122
2	50	5	15	38	32	81.5	49	124.5
2 1/2	65	6.5	16	40.5	33	84	50	127
3	75	7.5	17	43	34	86.5		
3 1/2	90	9	18	46	35	89		
4	100	10	19	48.5	36	91.5		
4 1/2	115	11.5	20	51	37	94		

KNITTING NEEDLES CONVERSION CHART

U.S.	0	1	2	3	4	5	6	7	8	9	10	10 1/2	11	13	15
Metric(mm)	2	2 1/4	2 3/4	3 1/4	3 1/2	3 3/4	4	4 1/2	5	5 1/2	6	6 1/2	8	9	10

CROCHET HOOKS CONVERSION CHART

U.S.	1/B	2/C	3/D	4/E	5/F	6/G	8/H	9/I	10/J	10 1/2/K	N
Continental-mm	2.25	2.75	3.25	3.5	3.75	4.25	5	5.5	6	6.5	9.0

Standard Yarn Weight System

Categories of yarn, gauge ranges, and recommended needle sizes

Yarn Weight Symbol & Category Names	1 SUPER FINE	2 FINE	3 LIGHT	4 MEDIUM	5 BULKY	6 SUPER BULKY
Type of Yarns in Category	Sock, Fingering, Baby	Sport, Baby	DK, Light Worsted	Worsted, Afghan, Aran	Chunky, Craft, Rug	Bulky, Roving
Knit Gauge* Ranges in Stockinette Stitch to 4 inches	21–32 sts	23–26 sts	21–24 sts	16–20 sts	12–15 sts	6–11 sts
Recommended Needle in Metric Size Range	2.25–3.25mm	3.25–3.75mm	3.75–4.5mm	4.5–5.5mm	5.5–8mm	8mm
Recommended Needle U.S. Size Range	1 to 3	3 to 5	5 to 7	7 to 9	9 to 11	11 and larger

* GUIDELINES ONLY: The above reflect the most commonly used gauges and needle sizes for specific yarn categories.

Special
Thanks

We would like to thank Plymouth Yarn Co. for providing all the yarn used in this book. We especially appreciate the help provided by JoAnne Turcotte. It's been great working with her. We would also like to thank the talented knitting designers whose work is featured in this collection.

Cindy Adams
Add a Little Glitter, 12
Garter-Stitch Gift Afghan, 157

Laura Andersson
Merry Cables, 8

Gayle Bunn
Fair Isle With Flair Set, 24

Anita Closic
Tie-It-On Scarf or Belt, 16
Felted Mittens, 66
Festive Felted Christmas Balls, 83
Christmas Rose, 113
Santa's Baby Blankie, 169

Ellen Edwards Drechsler
Peppermint Posers, 100

Donna Druchunas
Good Cheer Bottle Cozy, 35
Striped Gift Baskets, 39
Charming Button Bag, 43

Julie Gaddy
Felted Puppet Friends, 117
Glamour Throw for Grandma, 153

Sara Louise Harper
Don't Open 'til December 25, 61
Flurry of Fun Pillows, 94
Lacework Mantel Scarf, 99
Knitter's Christmas, 105
Cable-Rib Vest, 134
Dots-for-the-Daughters Pullover, 137
Candy Cane Cropped Cardie, 141
Plaid-to-Meet-You Throw, 162
Babes in Dreamland Blanket, 166
A Knitter's Tree Throw, 158

Debbie O'Neill
Holly Stocking Duo, 75

Kristin Omdahl
Magical Möbius, 48
Cable Your Wishes Pullover, 127
Cozy Throw for Grandpa, 149

Celeste Pinheiro
Soothing Spa Set, 36
Sweet Surprises, 63
Songbirds, 84
Great Bags for Giving, 91
Fascinating Hat & Handwarmers, 19

Posey Salem
Fashionably Fringed Tote, 40
Wrap as You Wish Capelet, 47
Wreath Table Trimmings, 88
Peppermint & Holly Doorstop, 103
Holly Days Throw, 147

Kathy Sasser
Accessorize Your Snowman, 114

Pauline Schultz
Luscious Warmth, 15
Chic Shrug, 44
Yuletide Jewels, 87

Scarlet Taylor
Razzle-Dazzle 'Em Stocking & Stars, 57
Cool Snowman & Santa Stockings, 68
Razzle-Dazzle Tree Skirt, 110
Snowflakes Hoodie, 122
Gift-Wrapped Cardigan & Headband, 131

Gaye Walker
Glorious Gift Throw, 161
Quick Festive Throw, 154

Christine L. Walter
Beaded Cable Head Cozy, 23
Not-Your-Basic Beanie, 31
Family Fun Mittens, 27
Quick Eyeglasses Case, 32
Socks in All Sizes,51
Felted Pot Cozies, 80

Lois S. Young
In the Spirit Scarf, 11

Diane Zangl
Tipsy Cables Throw, 165